Y0-ABB-687

THE TAO OF
ASIAN AMERICAN BELONGING

NO LONGER PROPERTY OF
SEATTLE PUBLIC LIBRARY

THE TAO OF ASIAN AMERICAN BELONGING

A Yinist Spirituality

by

YOUNG LEE HERTIG

ORBIS BOOKS

Maryknoll, New York 10545

Founded in 1970, Orbis Books endeavors to publish works that enlighten the mind, nourish the spirit, and challenge the conscience. The publishing arm of the Maryknoll Fathers and Brothers, Orbis seeks to explore the global dimensions of the Christian faith and mission, to invite dialogue with diverse cultures and religious traditions, and to serve the cause of reconciliation and peace. The books published reflect the views of their authors and do not represent the official position of the Maryknoll Society. To learn more about Maryknoll and Orbis Books, please visit our website at www.maryknollsociety.org.

Copyright © 2019 by Young Lee Hertig

Published by Orbis Books, Maryknoll, New York 10545-0302.

All rights reserved.

Chapter 4, "If I Perish, I Perish: Vashti and Esther," and Chapter 5, "The Dance of Encounter (John 4)," are reworked versions of the following published essays: "The Subversive Banquets of Vashti and Esther" and "Dialogical Encounters at the Well," in Young Lee Hertig and Chloe Sun, eds., *Mirrored Reflections: Reframing Biblical Characters* (Eugene, OR: Wipf & Stock, 2010), reprinted with permission of Wipf & Stock Publishing, www.wipfandstock.com. Chapter 9, "Asian American Women in the Workplace and the Church," was published in *People on the Way: Asian North Americans Discovering Christ, Culture, and Community*, ed. David Ng (Valley Forge, PA: Judson Press, 1996), 105-27. Reprinted with permission.

Scripture quotations are from the *New Revised Standard Version Bible*, copyright © 1989 National Council of the Churches of Christ in the United States of America, and the *New International Version Bible*, copyright © 1984 Zondervan House. Used by permission. All rights reserved worldwide.

No part of this publication may be reproduced or transmitted in any form or by any means, electronic or mechanical, including photocopying, recording or any information storage or retrieval system, without prior permission in writing from the publisher.

Queries regarding rights and permissions should be addressed to: Orbis Books, P.O. Box 302, Maryknoll, New York 10545-0302.

Manufactured in the United States of America.

Library of Congress Cataloging in Publication

Names: Hertig, Young Lee, 1954- author.
Title: The Tao of Asian American belonging : a yinist spirituality / by Young Lee Hertig.
Description: Maryknoll, NY : Orbis Books, [2019] | Summary: "This book expresses a quest for inclusion amid feminist, womanist, and mujerista discourses. Hertig's yinist spirituality is a novel attempt to lift up the voices of female, Asian American voices in Christian ecological theology. She coined the term yinist in the 1990s to "name the nameless Asian American feminism." The term yin refers to the feminine energy of Taoism, in contrast to the male yang. This book will be a valuable resource for the academy, churches, and denominational leaders"— Provided by publisher.
Identifiers: LCCN 2019004965 (print) | LCCN 2019980392 (ebook) | ISBN 9781626983359 (pbk.) | ISBN 9781608337996 (ebk.)
Subjects: LCSH: Christianity and other religions—Taoism. | Taoism—Relations—Christianity. | Asian American Christians—Religious life. | Christian women—Religious life—United States. | Yin-yang.
Classification: LCC BR128.T34 H47 2019 (print) | LCC BR128.T34 (ebook) | DDC 261.2/9514082—dc23
LC record available at https://lccn.loc.gov/2019004965
LC ebook record available at https://lccn.loc.gov/2019980392

Contents

Acknowledgments

I am deeply grateful to Orbis Books and my editor, Jill Brennan O'Brien, who perceived the significance of this book. The Maryknoll Sisters also understood and showed enthusiastic support when I presented the concept of yinist spirituality at the American Society of Missiology conference at Techny Towers, Ilinois, in 1998.

I wish to dedicate this book to my late mother, Jae Sook Shin, and to all the mothers who have deferred their dreams because of wars and conflicts and thus had to live vicariously through their children.

A word of thanks to my husband and partner, Paul Hertig, who has journeyed with me for more than three decades. I am grateful for his encouragement and accompaniment on this journey.

I am appreciative of the late Jung Young Lee, who pioneered Taoistic epistemology in his theological construction. This work is indebted to his pioneering creativity.

And finally, I want to thank Pete Hsu for his meticulous reading and invaluable feedback on the manuscript.

Introduction

The Tao of Asian American Belonging: A Yinist Spirituality originated from my quest for epistemic inclusion amid feminist, womanist, and mujerista discourses. Derived from Taoism, one of humankind's most sophisticated cosmologies, I coined the term *yinist* almost three decades ago to name the nameless Asian American feminist theology. The yinist paradigm I describe in this book can be applied across Asian American Christian theologies, but because I am speaking from an evangelical Christian context, I will emphasize its impact on Asian American evangelical Christians. The *yin* is the female principle that complements the *yang*, the male principle; in Taoist metaphysics, they form an indivisible whole. To remain nameless is to remain invisible and voiceless at the table and to be submerged among others' names. There is power in naming one's reality, which then allows us to engage in discourse at the table.

Ironically, my interest in Taoism began not in the East, but in the postmodern context of the West, when I explored a nondualistic but harmonious and ecoconscious feminism. "Yinist feminism diffuses false sets of dichotomy deriving from the dualistic paradigm: male against female, human being against nature, God apart from human being, this world apart from other world."[1] And it took a detour into quantum physics for me to justify the use of an Asian philosophical epistemology.

My encounter with Fritjof Capra's seminal book *The Tao of Physics*[2] was my initial entry point on the road to embracing

---

1. Young Lee Hertig, "The Asian-American Alternative to Feminism: A *Yinist* Paradigm," *Missiology: An International Review* 26, no. 1 (January 1998): 15.

2. Fritjof Capra, *The Tao of Physics: An Exploration of the Parallels*

Taoism as a theological paradigm. This led to other discoveries, such as Jung Young Lee's emphasis on cosmocentric anthropology and C.-S. Song's critique of Western reductionist theology. As Taoism provided an answer to Capra in explaining a *both/and* phenomenon in quantum physics, it also provided an alternative paradigm to the dissonant, reductionist Cartesian paradigm in the educational curriculum. Emboldened by the connection between quantum physics and Taoism, I began employing my term *yinist* in 1993 as a comprehensive and holistic paradigm of feminist Asian American theology. The term also provided me with an intrinsic category of belonging beyond the existing feminist discourses and amid emerging womanist and *mujerista* approaches.

Unlike feminists who propose additional terms, such as Rosemary Radford Ruether's *ecofeminism*, to address specific concerns, the term *yin*, the feminine energy of Taoism, is intrinsically comprehensive and holistic. I feel epistemological belonging when addressing yinist spirituality because of my lived experience of a holistic approach to health and nutrition. For many Asian Americans there is only a symbolic experience of Taoism in connection to nutrition and healing, such as in acupuncture and herbal medicine. Without knowledge of Taoist concepts, it is hard for Asian Americans to explicitly name the sources of their lived experiences of Taoism. There may even be some discomfort in using nonwhite knowledge for fear of triggering further marginalization as nonwhites.

Disclosing my own social and cultural locations as contact points with Taoism[3] is important because yinism is not only useful through my particular point of view; it embodies the kind of universality assumed by many Western theologies.

Yinist spirituality, therefore, is a search for an epistemological belonging and yearning to come to the table with a name tag. Compared to when I first introduced yinist spirituality in the 1990s, there seems to be an increasing acceptance of it among Asian American doctoral students today. This book could thus be

---

between Modern Physics and Eastern Mysticism (Boston: Shambhala Publications, 1975).

   3. And with process theology, as we will see in chapter 10.

valuable for the academy as well as for local churches of various denominations.

This book may also offer an educational process that connects mind, body, and action. Dichotomized Christian theology and its educational methods result in compartmentalization. Ill-equipped and mechanistically minded students are sent out into the field to do the ministry of organic human care. The holistic perspective of Taoism balances out yang-centered educational practices and norms that emphasize action and minimize introspection. In fact, digital technology dominates almost all spheres of human and institutional life, connecting people around the globe 24/7, and all the while, soulful spaces of mutual learning and mutual empowerment decrease in number and accessibility. We witness the dark side of our culture's fragmentation and extreme tribalism on a daily basis in the form of mass shootings, violence, sexual assault, and mental illness. It behooves us to offer a spirituality of harmony and to engage in a process that not only facilitates a more holistic educational process but also attends to the complexity of teaching and learning.

Defining the Term "Asian American"

The original meaning of the term "Asian American" dates back to the Asian American movement in the late 1960s during the civil rights era. The aim of the movement was to repudiate the alien label "Oriental" and to advocate for pan-Asian unity. Currently, the terms "Asian American" and "Asian and Pacific Islander American" are used to identify East Asians (Chinese, Japanese, and Korean), Central Asians (Pakistani, Afghan, and Burmese), South Asians (Indian), Southeast Asians (Thai, Vietnamese, Hmong, Cambodian, Laotian, Filipino, Malay, and Indonesian), and Pacific Islanders (Polynesian, Micronesian, and Melanesian).[4]

In this book, the term "Asian American" generally refers to Chinese, Japanese, Korean, and Vietnamese descendants whose

---

4. Timothy Tseng, "Pulpit and Pew Project," Research on Pastoral Leadership, Duke Divinity School, Durham, NC, 2005, available at www.pulpit andpew.org.

RELIGIOUS AFFILIATION OF ASIAN–AMERICAN SUBGROUPS

CHINESE AMERICANS

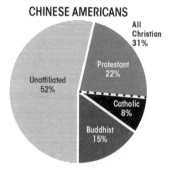

All Christian 31%
Protestant 22%
Unaffiliated 52%
Catholic 8%
Buddhist 15%

FILIPINO AMERICANS

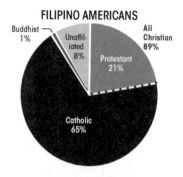

Buddhist 1%
Unaffiliated 8%
All Christian 89%
Protestant 21%
Catholic 65%

INDIAN AMERICANS

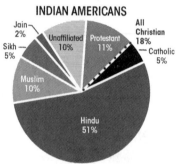

Jain 2%
Sikh 5%
Unaffiliated 10%
Protestant 11%
All Christian 18%
Catholic 5%
Muslim 10%
Hindu 51%

VIETNAMESE AMERICANS

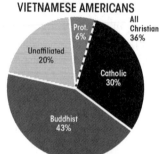

Prot. 6%
All Christian 36%
Unaffiliated 20%
Catholic 30%
Buddhist 43%

KOREAN AMERICANS

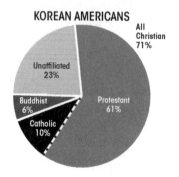

All Christian 71%
Unaffiliated 23%
Buddhist 6%
Catholic 10%
Protestant 61%

JAPANESE AMERICANS

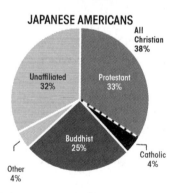

All Christian 38%
Unaffiliated 32%
Protestant 33%
Buddhist 25%
Catholic 4%
Other 4%

The "All Christian" category includes Protestants, Catholics and other Christians. Subgroups are listed in order of the size of the country-of-origin group in the total Asian-American population. Those who did not give an answer are not shown. Other religion, Hindu and Buddhist not shown for some subgroups. See topline in Appendix 4 for all responses. —PEW RESEARCH CENTER cultures have been impacted by the Confucian social hierarchy. The Asian American churches' organization conflates Confucian and Christian values. For Asian Americans' religious affiliations, the Pew Forum on "Asian Americans: A Mosaic of Faiths"[5] (see Figure 1) offers a rare view of Asian Americans' ethnicities and faith compositions.

Aims of the Book

This book's intended audience includes three constituencies. First, it serves as a textbook for graduate and undergraduate courses at seminaries and universities addressing gender and epistemic justice. Second, it supports the growing number of Asian American women clergy, ministry candidates, and denominational leaders across ecumenical and evangelical denominations in the United States and overseas. Third, it serves people who are concerned about creation care and gender equality, as well as those who are increasingly longing for holistic expressions of faith beyond the four walls of the church. In the midst of pseudo-masculine domination, women and nature are under assault. Meanwhile, Christianity also remains in a regressive state in the areas of gender equality/equity and sustainability. This extreme context demands an alternative epistemic lens for addressing faith, one that overcomes anthropocentric and masculine polarities. This book provides a resource for practitioners, missionaries, and pastor/scholars seeking an epistemological diversity that may expand their spiritual/theological practices.

Part One: An Asian American Alternative to Feminism

Part One introduces the holistic yinist epistemic lens as a way of articulating a spiritual belonging for Asians/Asian Americans that overcomes dichotomous epistemologies. The chapters in Part One introduce yinism in its derivation from yin, which is holistic,

---

5. "Asian Americans: A Mosaic of Faiths," Pew Forum on Religion and Public (July 19, 2012), http://www.pewforum.org.

xvi • *The Tao of Asian American Belonging*

dynamic, synthesizing, and complementary with yang, the male energy. Therefore, yinist feminism diffuses false sets of dichotomy that are derived from the dualistic paradigms of male against female, human being against nature, God apart from humans, and this world apart from the otherworldly. The yin and the yang are not separate, but complementary; one could not exist without the other. Together, they bring harmony to chaos.

Chapter 1: A Yinist Paradigm: Definitions and Perspectives

Chapter 1 proposes the yinist paradigm as a critique of reductionistic feminism. The feminist movement, despite its positive impact on women's status, is no exception to the dichotomous paradigm that works within a margin-vs.-center framework. Its epistemological lens is dualistic and thus divisive. Caught up in its reaction to male patriarchy, the feminist movement has not reconciled the intersecting relationships of gender, class, and race. For this reason, I do not feel connected to the word "feminist." I am unable to embrace all the issues that mainstream middle- and upper-class women have advocated for in seeking to represent women across all cultures and classes. It is no coincidence that contextualized feminist movements have developed, such as the African American womanist movement and the Latina women's *mujerista*. The yinist paradigm, representing Asian and Asian American women, is a necessary complement to these movements.

Chapter 1 also offers yinist definitions and perspectives. Because of the dominance of Eurocentric education, non-Western categories are foreign to most people in the United States, including Asian Americans. Therefore, Asian American experiences in family life and traditional Asian rituals often lack an understanding of the meanings behind familial rituals outside of the dominant American mainstream. By laying out the definitions and perspectives of the yinist paradigm from a Taoist philosophical perspective, this book will help readers to grasp both the meaning and the comprehensive implications of Taoism today.

Chapter 2: Why Asian/Asian American Theologies?

Chapter 2 addresses the question of why it is important to construct Asian American theologies. First of all, Asian American theologies have not been represented in theological discourses despite representing significant sources of inquiry. Second, Asian American seminarians who go through training in American seminaries today tend to find themselves ill-prepared when they start their ministry in Asian American churches. Third, "color- and culture-blind" theological education in general denies the innate Asian collective subconscious, which Jung Young Lee depicts with the yin/yang symbol. This denial, in turn, furthers the existing Asian American identity crisis.

Chapter 3: Spirituality and Ecology

Taoism can serve as one answer to our ecological crisis. Most Asian Americans educated in the United States have little exposure to innately Asian concepts, such as Taoism. Yet Taoism speaks to all areas of life, from ecology to diet. Its ancient, comprehensive cosmology is as relevant today as ever, especially as Mother Earth moans and groans under the weight of more than seven billion human inhabitants.

Therefore, exploring the origins of the Protestant disconnect between humanity and God on the one hand and the rest of God's creation on the other is a crucial step prior to recognizing the interwoven nature of all God's creation. It is also important to dialogue with womanist theology (e.g., Katie Cannon), metaphorical theological language (Sallie MacFague), ecofeminism (e.g., Rosemary Radford Ruether), and other areas of thought to show solidarity instead of remaining stuck in tribal divides. I do not wish Asian American women to perceive yinist epistemology as essentializing or ghettoizing. On the contrary, the yinist paradigm shares similar concerns with other movements that strive to retrieve the lost concept of ecological stewardship and humanity's responsibility as caretakers, not conquerors, of God's creation.

Part Two: Yinist Spirituality in the Bible

Part Two shows how approaching the biblical narratives from a both/and yinist lens rather than an either/or lens illuminates fresh understandings of biblical characters such as Queen Vashti and Esther, the Samaritan woman, Hellenist widows, and the concept of becoming the body of Christ. For textual reasons, I use both the New Revised Standard Version (NRSV) and the New International Version (NIV) of the Bible for scripture quotations in this book.

Chapter 4: "If I Perish, I Perish": Vashti and Esther

Chapter 4 interprets the two queens in the book of Esther as two sides of one woman working toward a journey of wholeness. The two women both exude the spirituality of letting go that results in life-giving twists and turns.

Chapter 5: The Dance of Encounter (John 4)

Chapter 5 investigates Jesus's transforming power, a power that often resides in his authentic vulnerability. In a culture of hyper-masculinity, a yinish vulnerability as a spiritual leader's power in ministry is much needed. In a dialogical encounter initiated by Jesus, a woman with no name who is shunned in her village finds her personhood and connects with the image of God in her. The intersectional "-isms" of race, ethnicity, class, gender, religion, and region are transcended in this dialogue. As a result, the woman is restored and liberated.

As Paulo Freire emphasized, each person's ontological vocation is to identify one's calling and to become more human. The Samaritan woman is liberated from being an *object* of oppression to become a *subject* of liberation. No longer objectified, she instead becomes an actor and a transformer of lives, both her own life and the life of her village. This transformation also awaits many Asian American women today.

I also honor my own cherished mentor, Dr. Paul Hiebert, in this chapter.

Chapter 6: Cross-Cultural Mediation (Acts 6)

Chapter 6 proposes and elaborates on the premise that mediating conflicts must supersede any other means of addressing conflict, including our most common fallbacks of avoidance and violence. This chapter highlights the qualifications of third-party mediators who rise above the yin and yang of conflict, thus contributing to the vitality of the mission of the church.

Intergroup conflict, such as that found in the contemporary church, is addressed in chapter 6 through an analysis of the apostles in Acts. Having gone through persecution in Acts 5, the apostles are confronted with an intergroup conflict in Acts 6 in the form of the exclusion of Hellenist Jewish widows from the daily distribution of food. This exclusion exacerbates the existing tension between the Hebraic Jews and the Jewish diaspora in a rapidly Hellenizing world. There is a powerful parallel to the world we live in today, which is characterized by an increasing number of displaced migrants and refugees in a globalized planet—a situation that emboldens extremist reactionaries.

In the midst of such epochal change, the core beliefs of the Hebrews are challenged from every direction, which intensifies their impulse to protect their beliefs, identity, and sense of belonging. In this context, leadership that diffuses conflict rather than escalates it matters greatly. This chapter examines how the apostles handle a complicated intergroup conflict.

Chapter 7: Becoming the Body of Christ (1 Corinthians 12)

The apostle Paul's metaphor of becoming the "body of Christ" illustrates perspectives from general systems theory, German *gestalt*, and yinist spirituality. Depicting the process by which parts become the whole body, this chapter connects a yinist perspective to the concept of becoming the body of Christ. One key requirement of wholeness resides in affirmative action that cedes to the weaker part in order to equalize power. Beyond the church, 1 Corinthians 12 can also be usefully applied in today's world xx • *The Tao of Asian American Belonging*

to show what it means to collaborate and partner with different "parts" in order to build a greater whole.

Part Three: Contemporary Embodiments of Yinist Spirituality

Part Three focuses on examples of yinist spirituality from contemporary Asian and Asian American contexts in order to illustrate its embodiment and applicability.

Chapter 8: "If I Perish, I Perish": Maria Kim and Yu Kwan Soon

The purpose of this chapter is to name two historic Korean Christian women leaders, Maria Kim and Yu Kwan Soon, whose faith and nonviolent resistance against Japanese colonization exemplify the spirituality of "if I perish, I perish" (Esther 4:16).

Documenting Kim's and Yu's stories in English is much needed, because Asian Americans unfortunately often are ignorant of the historical roots of their faith. March 1, 2019, marked the centennial of the Korean independence movement. The movement leaders found their courage in the stories of the prophet Jeremiah and Joan of Arc, which then emboldened their resistance. Totally unarmed, these women resistors demonstrated fearless leadership in confronting the heavily armed colonizer. Firearms and tanks could not defeat their courage and relentless faith in God. Kim and Yu exemplified a paradoxical duality of yinish surrender and yangish resistance. The dialectical duality of pacifistic inner surrender to death (yin) and subversive outer resistance (yang/animus) exemplifies the holistic spirituality of yin/yang.

Chapter 9: Asian American Women in the Workplace and the Church

The feminist movement does not fully capture the hearts of Asian American women—despite the importance of gender equality to them—because multiple marginalities alienate us in our homes, churches, and workplaces. Without a name, Asian American women are apt to be theological and cultural orphans. This chapter gives voice to the peculiar struggles of Asian American women on the front lines of Christian leadership, covering real-life narratives from a yinist spiritual perspective. Estranged from the feminist movement and blocked by our own ethnic groups, we women of Asian heritage seek our own identity and integrity, our own call to being. Once we feel anchored, we will then be able to engage with divergent voices.

Chapter 10: Imagining a Yinist Embodiment of Asian American Churches

This final chapter envisions a more equal pulpit in Asian American churches. The exclusion of women's voices from the pulpit continues to marginalize women, labeling them as second class. I believe that male dominance of the pulpit in Asian American churches perpetuates the masculinization of Christian faith and life, and also distorts the gospel message. Fidelity to the gospel and the fullness of the body of Christ requires that churches be provided with resources to unmask patriarchal hermeneutics and to implement gender inclusivity in Asian American pulpits. Gender inclusivity in the pulpit would ultimately serve both genders, because such an inclusion would result in a healthy body of Christ. I dare to dream and imagine this whole and equal inclusivity implemented widely across mainline and evangelical churches in the United States.

• PART ONE •

An Asian American Alternative to Feminism

A Yinist Paradigm

Definitions and Perspectives

The Indian theologian Sunand Sumithra once remarked, "We Indian people are tired of theological answers to questions we never raised."[1] These words resonate as artificially constructed boundaries between margin and center continue to reveal the dichotomous lens through which we see reality. Jesus, the suffering servant of Galilee, set the world free from the myth of differentiation between the powerful elite and the powerless masses. Jesus, once and for all time, abolished top–down power dynamics. Jesus lived among and identified with Galileans, people who suffered throughout history because of marginalizing invasions and oppression.[2] It was there

---

1. Sunand Sumithra and I were global research scholars at Fuller Theological Seminary from 1996 to 1998. One day, I saw Sumithra packing all of his books. He said that he was going back to India rather than finishing his trilogy on systematic theology, and went to articulate succinctly the problem of writing systematic theology based on Western problems and issues. Although Sumithra has since passed away, what he shared at that moment still stays with me.

2. Richard Horsley states that "Galilee was repeatedly subjected by a succession of outside rulers, usually from the great empires. Yet the Galilean people had a keen sense of independence, periodically resisting or outright revolting against those rulers, whose regimes were usually based in faraway capitals"; see Richard A. Horsley, *Galilee: History, Politics, People* (Valley Forge, PA: Trinity Press International, 1995), 276. In fact, there is archaeological evidence that Galilee was both devastated and almost entirely depopulated by the Assyrians in 733–732 BCE (ibid., 26).

in Galilee that Jesus set up his ministry, shattering the marginalized status of Galileans and invalidating the perceived center of religious life. Jesus's journeys in and around Galilee and Jerusalem offer insight into the obliteration of the socially constructed wall between the margin and the center today.

The dualistic epistemological trap of either/or, powerful/powerless, and center/margin conditions people to think in terms of contrast and differences. However, no one has the right to affirm his or her identity by denying the worthiness of others. "I am not those others" is a destructive and separatist use of power.[3] When our epistemological lens itself is hierarchically bound and we use it to address the center/margin dichotomy, we are ill-equipped to even diagnose the problem, much less solve it.

The preliminary question then is: How can we overcome the dichotomy between center and margin when we limit our dialogue to the polarizing, dualistic lens of the margin versus the center?

Critique of Reductionist Feminism

The feminist movement, despite its positive impact on women's status, is no exception to the dichotomous paradigm that works within a center/margin framework. Its epistemological lens is dualistic, and thus divisive. Caught up in its reaction to patriarchy, the feminist movement has not reconciled the intersecting relationships of gender, class, and race.

For this reason, I do not feel connected to the word *feminist*. I am unable to embrace all the issues that mainstream middle- and upper-class women have advocated for in seeking to represent women across all cultures and classes. And I am not alone in my feeling of disconnect. Several contextualized feminist movements have developed, such as the African American womanist and Latina women's *mujerista* theologies.

What then shall we call the Asian women's feminism? I had been thinking about the nameless Asian women's struggle for a long

---

3. Kathryn Tanner, *The Politics of God* (Minneapolis, MN: Fortress Press, 1992), 213–15.

time and wanted to provide a name that represents our history and context while also connecting us with our primordial archetype. The word *yinist* popped into my head one day and filled the void. It is taken from the word *yin,* the female energy in Taoism. This female energy is comprehensive because it encompasses gender, ecology, nature, health, and God. The yin is holistic, dynamic, synthesizing, and complementary with yang, the male energy. Yinist feminism, therefore, diffuses false dichotomies deriving from the dualistic paradigm: male against female, humanity against nature, God apart from humanity, this world apart from the other world.[4]

Yin and yang imbalance exists among elite women whose ideas are labeled progressive. Mainstream feminism, initiated by the white upper-middle-class, arose as a reaction against hierarchical patriarchy. But in some aspects, it inherited a form of patriarchy (with its emphasis on masculine characteristics) by replacing male dominance with female dominance. And like patriarchal exclusiveness, white feminism practices similar exclusiveness based on cultural and social conformity. At times I wonder if there is any difference between the male hierarchy and the female hierarchy. Mere gender rotation within the same hierarchical system is equally exclusive and oppressive. If the dominant power holder is simply replaced, there is no liberation or transformation. Classism and racism among feminists cannot be overcome unless the unfamiliar other is included in the circle of mainstream feminism. The limited experiences of white women should not represent the realities of all women. As our Brazilian sister Ivone Gebara points out with regard to exclusivity within feminist movements, "We have to admit that small groups have a small history and if they want to spread their influence more than just for the present generation they have to be better institutionalized and include more diversity."[5]

The assimilation of white feminist norms and values provides

---

4. This dialectic interdependence is expressed in the creation story of male and female in Genesis 1:27.
5. Ivone Gebara, "Feminism and Religious Identity," Pat Reif Memorial Lecture delivered at Claremont College, March 2009, https://www.womens ordination.org/2008/08/23/feminism-and-religious-identity-by-ivone-gebara/.

little space for nonwhite women. Representing silenced voices and groups is crucial because oppression is cultural, social, and religious. Jung Young Lee stresses the problem of uniformity: "If I cannot appreciate different colors, I want to be color-blind."[6] Furthermore, he critiques the inevitable rut produced by a centralist ideology: "When centralist ideology is normative, everyone wants to be at the center. The center's power, wealth, and glory pull people like a magnet. The margins as a symbol of the weak, poor, and despised repel people."[7]

As long as yang is at the center, dominating all spheres of human life, even feminists are tempted to emulate yang energy by placing themselves at the center. In doing this, yin is further marginalized and silenced. The response to white feminism by nonwhite women is either avoidance or separation; this response divides women and eliminates the opportunity for true dialogue.

Asian women pioneers in theological circles confront nothing but obstacles. Asian patriarchs resist female leadership by Asian women while accepting white women's leadership because of their "safe" cultural distance. Mainstream institutions can generally hide behind the rhetoric of cultural correctness while choosing the voice of the Asian male's power structure. Furthermore, even a large number of Asian women, familiar with the male image of leadership, often resist the unfamiliar female image of leadership and dismiss female leaders because they do not want to see other women play a role they themselves do not exercise.

How then can all women from different contexts equally share in one another's particularities and commonalities as human beings? What keeps women of all races from engaging in authentic encounters? In this book, I attempt to answer these questions by challenging a binary epistemology based on contrasts. I seek to return to an epistemology of wholeness through the harmonious balance between and beyond yin and yang. Both qualities of yin

---

6. Jung Young Lee, *Marginality: The Key to Multicultural Theology* (Minneapolis, MN: Fortress Press, 1995), 29.

7. Ibid., 150.

and yang within women and men should be balanced within and between gender, race, class, and religion.

A Yinist Feminism: The Harmonious Chaos of Women

The yin-and-yang paradigm loosens the gridlock of center versus margin. Jesus, throughout the gospels, models this balance. He pays attention to the marginalized, thus lifting up their voices.

The Chinese were attentive to nature because the livelihood of farmers depended on nature. The yin and yang concept thus developed through their observation of nature.

Yin	Yang
earth	heaven
moon	sun
night	day
winter	summer
autumn	spring
moisture	dryness
coolness	warmth
interior	surface

Figure 1. Yin and yang contrasts in nature

The elaborate observation of nature through the lens of yin and yang has been extensively chronicled. A. C. Graham invites us to explore this aspect of Chinese cosmology:

> Of the ch'i inclining to Heaven, the raging became wind; of the combining ch'i of Heaven and Earth, the harmonious became rain. When *yin* and *yang* clashed, being roused they became thunder, crossing paths they became lightning, confusing they became mist. When the *yang* ch'i prevailed, it scattered to become rain and dew; when the *yin* ch'i prevailed, it congealed to become frost and snow.[8]

---

8. A. C. Graham, *Yin-Yang and the Nature of Correlative Thinking* (Kent Ridge, Singapore: Institute of East Asian Philosophies, 1986), 31.

The harmonious dynamic between yin and yang is symbolized by the life-giving rain. Yet, we notice here the indication of variables in the inner/outer dynamics of yin and yang: rage, clash, arousal, crossing, and confusion. The Chinese interpretation of natural phenomena through the window of yin and yang energy (ch'i) in nature provides us with ample implications for human dynamics. The poetic images evoked by Jo Ana Smith depicts the dynamism of yin and yang reflected in nature:

> In the beginning the creation goddess gave birth to both Light and Dark. Light and Dark loved the goddess and vied for her attention. Each one thought it was the better. Dark competed with Light. Light wanted to change Dark. For many moons they struggled against each other causing conflict and distress . . . until they crumbled with exhaustion. During their time of letting go both Light and Dark cast their gaze upon the moon and saw the moon was both Light and Dark. Light looked at Dark and recognized itself. . . . Dark looked at Light and recognized itself . . . and in that moment of recognition there was Unity and Harmony.[9]

The above description of harmony in the midst of chaos is indicative of yinist feminism. Yin and yang are two sides of one coin. Chaos itself holds the key to harmony since harmony contains chaos. This contrasts with the linear Western concept of order in which chaos and harmony are mutually exclusive.

Yin and Yang in Human Nature

As yin and yang dynamics exist in nature, so they do in human nature as well.

The following chart illustrates yin and yang in human dynamics:[10]

---

9. Jo Ana Smith was a student enrolled in a class entitled "Women Doing Faith-based Social Analysis" at Immaculate Heart College Center in Los Angeles, CA. Following my lecture on yinist feminism, she recited this poem spontaneously.

10. Figure 2 is modeled on Fritjof Capra, *The Turning Point: Science, Society, and the Rising Culture* (Toronto: Bantam Books, 1983), 38.

Yin	Yang
feminine	masculine
contractive	expansive
conservative	demanding
responsive	aggressive
cooperative	competitive
intuitive	rational
synthesizing	analytic

Figure 2. Yin and yang contrasts in human beings

Austrian American physicist Fritjof Capra articulates the complementary nature of yin and yang in human beings.[11] However, he laments the fact that throughout human civilization, yang-driven culture swallowed yinish culture. Despite the current Western awakening to Chinese philosophy, Capra argues that the West has never understood the yin and yang concepts in the Chinese sense. Capra gives credit to author and professor Manfred Porkert for his comprehensive interpretation of the concept through the study of Chinese medicine. The Chinese diagnosed human pathology holistically based on the dynamic balance between yin and yang, observing that their imbalance caused harm and sickness. This dynamic balance, essential within human physiology, also applies to human social dynamics. Yinist feminism thus seeks the balance of yin and yang in society.

The Harmful Imbalance of Yin and Yang

Human culture has identified maleness with yang exclusively and femaleness with yin exclusively. However, both male and female have yin and yang energies. Yinist feminism as a theology of balance is twofold in nature. First, yin and yang are both male and female. One reaches the fullness of humanity when he or she identifies both yin and yang within himself or herself. However, yin in male and yin in female are not the same. Jungian psychology

11. Ibid., 36.

uses the term *anima* to describe the inner feminine within a man. Likewise, the concept of *animus* refers to Jung's theory of the inner masculine within a woman.

Second, once it is understood that yin and yang are found in both male and female, the extreme polarization of male *as yang* and female *as yin* will be balanced. Without this balancing, the overdose of either one causes disease. Both females and males suffer from this polarization, and many Asian American women in particular struggle with an overdose of yin because of Asian cultural values.

Many Asian American Christian women suffer from a double dose of yin ideals from male-dominated cultural and theological values. Asian American Christian women are often surrounded with messages from the pulpit, their husbands, and their mothers-in-law, leading them to be sacrificial, cross bearing, and nameless. This double dose of yin from the culture and from Christianity leaves Asian American women without an outlet, which results in emotional and physical wounds. The Asian American women's image of Jesus reflects this extreme imbalance. Whenever I ask Korean American Christian women about the qualities of Jesus, they list nothing but yinish characteristics such as mercy, humility, softness, gentleness, compassion, and forgiveness, mirroring their own lives. On the other hand, many Western men and women list both yin and yang qualities in their images of Jesus.

Many second-generation daughters often bear anger on behalf of their mothers, who live with abuse, suffering, and pain inflicted by the extreme yang characteristics embodied by their fathers. These inequities continue into the next generation, furthering the imbalance of yin-and-yang dynamics in immigrant family life.

Extremity and Reversal

The polarized representation of yin and yang around gender stereotypes impoverishes humanity and inflicts harm. In the modern industrial society, yang energy dominates, and thus society expects women to fit the yinish stereotype by polarizing what is intrinsically two sides of one coin. The healthy human being cannot stand on the fragmented extreme of either the yang-based or the yin-based life.

Lao Tzu's philosophy, Taoism, illuminates this lack of balance in the way we confront contemporary problems. Yang-driven values dominate our lives in the city, the *polis*, which from the Greco-Roman period was considered the male domain, while the *oikos* (household) was seen as the female domain.[12]

From escalating gun violence to the idealization of profit making, the destructiveness of the yang-driven mentality is peaking. In an ever-expanding battle zone, human lives disappear in an increasing tide of violence. Is this an indication that a reversal of this extremity is around the corner? The media permeate mainstream culture, feeding violence and numbing our senses and souls as human beings. Is the world capable of feeling anymore? Is it even capable of dreaming anymore?

These questions are at the core of a struggle to seek balance in a world of extreme imbalance. *The Book of Changes* describes nature as follows: "When the sun has reached its meridian, it declines, and when the moon has become full, it wanes."[13] Therefore, Lao Tzu describes the movement of Tao as "reversal."[14] The concept of reversals permeates biblical accounts as well. Matthew introduces Jesus's ministry with a reversal that is also cited in Isaiah 9: "the people who sat in darkness have seen a great light, and for those who sat in the region and shadow of death light has dawned" (Matthew 4:16).

Jesus's ministry in first-century Galilee occurred when the gap between the rich and the poor was at an extreme. Herod's reign

12. Karen Jo Torjesen, *When Women Were Priests: Women's Leadership in the Early Church and the Scandal of Their Subordination in the Rise of Christianity* (New York: HarperCollins Publishers, 1993), 6.

13. Fung Yu-Lan, *A Short History of Chinese Philosophy: A Systematic Account of Chinese Thought from Its Origins to the Present Day* (New York: Free Press, 1948), 19.

14. Ibid.

was "extremely oppressive on the ordinary people of the land."[15] In Mary's Magnificat, the mighty and the rich are brought down and sent away empty while the humble and the hungry are exalted and filled. The reversal in Mary's song results in yang's extremity:

> He has brought down the powerful from their thrones,
> and lifted up the lowly;
> He has filled the hungry with good things,
> and sent the rich away empty. (Luke 1:52–53)

The dominance of yang without the balance of yin drives yang to its peak and heightens the hierarchy of racism, sexism, and classism. Driven by ego-bounded competition and expansionism, the overdose of yang results in massive oppression of and violence toward living organisms and the earth. Thus, yinist spirituality seeks to process multiple dimensions of relationships and their mutual interconnectedness with God, humanity, nature, and the ecological environment. In the midst of chaotic pain, yinist spirituality embraces an inner and outer harmony because yin and yang, dialectically interdependent, balance the imbalanced. The process of balancing cannot avoid a reactionary response prior to the balanced harmony.

The replacement of men with women as the dominant power does not improve the conditions of life; what matters is balance. Jerome Neyrey suggests that the purpose of reversals in Luke-Acts was to rearrange "the perceived map which indicated who enjoyed God's favor and who was in the inner circle of God's elect" by including the dishonored and the unclean.[16] Therefore, Neyrey prefers the words *inclusivity* and *impartiality* to *reversal*.[17] Neyrey has identified the essence of biblical reversals as balancing the imbalanced.

15. Sean Freyne, *The Jesus Movement and Its Expansion: Meaning and Mission* (Grand Rapids: William B. Eerdmans, 2014), 117.

16. Jerome H. Neyrey, "The Symbolic Universe of Luke-Acts," in *The Social World of Luke-Acts: Models of Interpretation*, ed. Jerome H. Neyrey (Peabody, MA: Hendrickson Publishers, 1991), 297.

17. Ibid.

Yinist Feminism as a Theology of Harmony

The Bible is full of opposites existing in harmony. Benedictine Sister Joan Chittister articulates the harmonious dynamics of yin and yang through the spirituality of embrace. She writes, "Scripture is full of the coming together of opposites—Joseph and his brothers, Moses's mother and Pharaoh's daughter, Jesus and the Samaritan woman, the young woman Mary and the old woman Elizabeth."[18]

Yinist feminism seeks coexistence without male or female domination. Beneath the scenic order of the status quo is an undercurrent of pain and chaos. Dialectically, within this undercurrent of chaos one can find internal order. Chaos itself holds the key to harmony. If one enters the chaos, one just might discover a new order. This dual perspective has given hope to the Chinese people to overcome a long history of hard times. During peaceful times, Chinese people are cautious of danger; during dangerous times, they anticipate peace.

The postmodern atmosphere has allowed some white sisters to turn their eyes beyond the Western paradigm to ecofeminism, but the corresponding asymmetries of a yin and yang cosmology are more comprehensive than the current movement of ecofeminism. Yinist feminism as a paradigm encompasses contextual and epistemological particularity, yet shares universality in the cosmological pattern.

Yinist feminism is ecologically and spiritually connected. It seeks harmony, but not without chaos. Yinist feminism accepts the dialectic tension between harmony and conflict. Its epistemology allows interconnectedness between the paradox of order and chaos. Therefore, it seeks to understand reality through the lens of integrated wholes whose properties cannot be reduced to those of smaller units. Yinist feminism is thus nonlinear and dynamic. It understands nature as a dynamically interconnected network of relationships that include the human observer as an integral component. In this regard, yinist feminism corresponds to ecofeminism

---

18. Joan Chittister, *For Everything a Season* (Maryknoll, NY: Orbis Books, 1995), 102.

in its emphasis on mutual interconnectedness between human beings and their ecological environment.

We have observed a rich parallel between Galileans and Asian American women. Asian American women who do not fit the Asian American women's stereotype (that is, submissive humility) have several strikes against them. Like Galileans, we too have to battle against people's assumptions and expectations based on the dichotomy of center and margin.[19] We must battle against the passive, submissive, and obedient stereotype, both from within the community and from the mainstream culture. Simultaneously, we have to create a new category because we tread on a path without road signs or maps. In our vulnerability, our dependence on God's providence becomes our sole assurance. We are accustomed to lacking affirmation from either the Asian American or the mainstream community. We experience the exception to the rule as our common rule. Through this, we learn to harmonize chaos as an integral aspect of our daily routine. Thus, we Asian American women are yinist.

---

19. Galilean Jews of the first century were known to be in conflict with Jerusalem temple authorities who expected Galilean Jews to follow their laws and give tithes and offerings to the temple and the priesthood (Horsley, *Galilee*, 139, 156, 157). However, the Galilean Jews maintained a certain amount of independence (238, 276). Galileans were also known to rise up against political domination in their region (181).

· 2 ·

Why Asian/Asian American Theologies?

The issue of whose story gets told and accepted by a society and whose stories are suppressed or simply not told, is important, for those who "tell the story" are able to shape people's actions, ideas, and values, and identities in all sorts of significant ways.

Joanne D. Birdwhistell[1]

Why construct Asian American theologies, and Asian American evangelical theologies in particular? I propose four responses to this question. First, Asian American theologies (especially evangelical theologies) have not been represented in theological discourse, even though a large percentage of Asian American Christians are evangelical.[2] Second, Asian American seminarians who go through training in American seminaries today tend to find themselves ill prepared when they start their ministry in Asian American churches. Third, color- and culture-blind theological education in general denies the innate Asian collective subconscious, which Jung

---

1. Joanne D. Birdwhistell, "Ecological Questions for Daoist Thought: Contemporary Issues and Ancient Texts," in *Daoism and Ecology: Ways within a Cosmic Landscape*, ed. N. J. Girardot, James Miller, and Liu Xiao-gan (Cambridge, MA: Harvard University Press, 2001), 25.

2. "America's Changing Religious Landscape," Pew Research Center, May 12, 2015, http://www.pewforum.org.

15

Young Lee depicts with the yin/yang symbol. This, in turn, furthers the existing Asian American identity crisis.

Lee contrasts differing worldviews of the East and West:

> While the West is interested in an anthropocentric approach to cosmology, East Asia is more interested in a cosmocentric approach to anthropology. In East Asia, anthropology is a part of cosmology; a human being is regarded as a microcosm of the cosmos. The inseparable relationship between humanity and the world is a distinctive characteristic of East Asian philosophy.[3]

The West and the Western paradigm emphasize a Cartesian view, relegating other streams of philosophy—as represented by such figures as Arthur Schopenhauer, Friedrich Nietzsche, Ludwig Wittgenstein, and Capra—to the background (in the yin position). I am not arguing for a polarized view of the East and West, but rather for an acknowledgment of the similarities of the two by unpacking the fusion of horizons shared by Taoism and Celtic spirituality.

The fourth and final reason why Asian American theologies need to be constructed lies in the current pastoral leadership crisis in the Asian American evangelical church. The lack of theological, cultural, and personal identities integrating Asian American evangelical experiences poses a serious problem for the future of the Asian American evangelical church. Despite the vitality of the pan-Asian American congregational trend, an effort toward Asian American theological construction will define who we are as *Asian*, *American*, and *evangelical*.

Out of such hunger for an innate Asian collective consciousness, I turn to both Taoism and Celtic spirituality. Both traditions share holistic worldviews that can balance yang-dominant values, an extreme that harms all sectors of living organisms. Taoism confronts Confucian corruption; Celtic spirituality confronts Roman imperial expansion. Behind every sealed orthodoxy stand margin-

---

3. Jung Young Lee, *The Trinity in Asian Perspective* (Nashville, TN: Abingdon Press, 1996), 18.

alized voices that deserve recognition since their voices, after all, could have balanced the extremes of a school of thought.

Therefore, I categorize both Taoism and Celtic spirituality as yinist, the feminine energy of Taoism, in order to move yang (male energy) to the background and yin (female energy) to the foreground. This does not mean that the yinist paradigm excludes yang, but that the dynamic of the two is dual, though not dualistic. The term yinist parallels the terms ecofeminist and womanist.

The yinist, female energy in Taoism is comprehensive because it encompasses gender, ecology, nature, health, and God. The yin is holistic, dynamic, synthesizing, and complementary with yang, the male energy. Yinist feminism, therefore, diffuses false dichotomies deriving from the dualistic paradigm: male against female, humanity against nature, god apart from humanity, this world apart from the other world.

In the face of global homogenization of human culture around "maximum profit," our world begs for a paradigm change, not merely a programmatic one. The yinist paradigm can overcome what Paul G. Hiebert identifies as a two-tiered, Neoplatonic theology of religion and science that creates an excluded middle.[4] In the West, this middle level formerly offered guidance for the unknown future, the crises of present life, and the unknown past. It began disappearing in the seventeenth and eighteenth centuries when the world was divided into poles: Cartesian dualism/scientific empiricism versus religion. The consequence of this polemic worldview includes secularization on the one hand and the rise of the evangelical charismatic movement on the other.

In the absence of holistic theologies, the emerging generation, in their hunger for filling the void of the excluded middle, turns to charismatic expressions of faith in reaction to rationalistic Cartesian theologies. In a roundtable conversation with second-generation Korean American seminarians at Fuller Theological Seminary, I learned how much they yearn for guidance, authentic community, and caring mentors from the first generation. Unfortunately,

---

4. Paul G. Hiebert, *Anthropological Reflections on Missiological Issues* (Grand Rapids: Baker Books, 1994), 196–97.

their first-generation leaders are often unavailable because they are caught up with modernistic and Confucian models of ministry—building projects, performance, and the size of their congregations. The second-generation longs for a Christianity that embodies authentic relationship rather than performance, inner landscape rather than outer accomplishment. A holistic theological paradigm can fill the void of the emerging generation.

One of the reasons why so many Asian American Christians are evangelical relates to the persistence of an internalized evangelical faith that had been instilled in the Western mission movement at the turn of the twentieth century. Another reason could be a fusion of Asian Confucian fundamentalism with Christian fundamentalism. Under such belief systems, Asian American Christians remain culturally and racially silenced. The faith of the first generation, separated from daily life, reflects alienation from the mainstream culture. And upon experiencing a glass ceiling in the corporate world, the English-speaking generations return to their ethnic enclave.

I use the plural term *theologies* rather than the singular *theology* assuming that all theological constructions derive from a particular context that shares commonalities with all theologies while also containing particularities. What shapes the hermeneutical approach of a theologian depends on personal, cultural, and social locations. Without exception, I bring my multiple hybridity as Korean, American, female, wife, mother, instructor, and itinerant pastor, who is both evangelical and ecumenical. I also bring a daily encounter of heightened consciousness of race, class, and gender as well as the constant reminder of being an *alien Other,* as described by Edward Said. In his critique of the terms *Orient, Oriental, and Orientalism,* Said points out the underlying assumption of the West that sees non-Western as alien Other. Hence, he argues:

> My contention is that without examining Orientalism as a discourse one cannot possibly understand the enormously systematic discipline by which European culture was able to manage—and even to produce—the Orient politically, socio-

logically, militarily, ideologically, scientifically, and imaginatively during the post-Enlightenment period.[5]

It could seem difficult to connect Christianity, particularly the evangelical tradition, to an innate Asian culture that can easily be labeled "nonevangelical" or even "liberal," if not *alien*. One might ask, for example, how Taoist hermeneutics can be considered evangelical. Nevertheless, as much as Christianity has been Romanized, and thus Westernized, it can also be Asianized without compromising the biblical metanarrative that cuts across particularities of culture, race, gender, class, time, and space.

From an evangelical perspective, I connect deeply with the nineteenth-century legacy of Charles Finney's movement that embodied "the spirit of revivalism and reform." I also find kinship with Oberlin College's history of confronting the difficult issues of race, slavery, women, and a host of other issues. Oberlin College exemplifies holistic theologies in action that can balance our disembodied, two-tiered evangelical theology, rooted in the Enlightenment paradigm. Finally, I appreciate Donald Dayton's documentation of our amazing evangelical heritage. The fact that black students boarded and roomed with whites before the Civil War era offers timeless inspiration.

All three of these (Finney, Oberlin, and Dayton) were refreshing voices in the religious establishment, and they were committed to universal morality—that is, the equality of all human beings, the recognition of chaos both within human nature and in nature, and the emphasis on wisdom over dogma. The epistemological convergence of Taoism and Celtic spirituality shares the universal connection of two distant lands from which emerged very similar views around the same time in history.

The purpose of this chapter, therefore, is to provide a "third-eye perspective," as C.-S. Song calls it.[6] By looking at the fusion of two

---

5. Edward Said, *Orientalism* (New York: Vintage Books: A Division of Random House, 1979), 3.

6. C.-S. Song, *Third-Eye Theology: Theology in Formation in Asian Settings* (Maryknoll, NY: Orbis Books, 1979).

horizons—Asian Taoism and Western Celtic spirituality—I seek to construct a holistic Asian American evangelical theology, which I name yinist. My fascination with Taoist and Celtic spirituality comes from today's dire context, in which religion fuels violence and the pursuit of maximum profit threatens the sustainability of all living organisms. As Hans Küng stresses, there can be no peace in the world unless there is peace among religions.

I use the term Asian American to refer mainly to Chinese, Japanese, and Korean descendants whose cultures have been impacted by the Confucian social hierarchy. The organized Asian American churches conflate Confucian and Christian values. Although Confucianism also influences Vietnamese culture, because of my limited cultural contact with the Vietnamese, I will generally use the term Asian American to refer to East Asian descendants.

The Historical Context of Taoism

How do ancient paradigms relate to today's context, particularly to Asian American evangelicals? I find history dialectically repetitious. The resurgence of Celtic spirituality and the Western fascination with Eastern thought in our postmodern setting testify to a contemporary reaction to extreme modernity. Kristopher Schipper argues that the context from which Taoism emerged is not a remote place but the highly developed region of Shu in northern Sichuan where advanced hydraulic mechanisms were first utilized in agriculture. This development paralleled an economic exploitation that fueled military expansion. Schipper describes the socio-economic conditions of Shu:

> All the endemic ills connected with sedentary life and high economical pressure, the scourges of rural China, were experienced there: abusive taxation, raids by external nomadic tribes, high population density, epidemics, and famine.[7]

---

7. Kristopher Schipper, "Daoist Ecology: The Inner Transformation. A Study of the Precepts of the Early Daoist Ecclesia," in *Daoism and Ecology: Ways within a Cosmic Landscape*, ed. N. J. Girardot, James Miller, and Liu Xiaogan (Cambridge, MA: Harvard University Press, 2001), 82–83.

Against both human and environmental corruption, Taoism arose and provided spiritual sanctuary for the people in crisis in China. On a much larger scale than what the ancient Chinese faced, today's world, dominated by globalization and hyperdevelopment, produces catastrophic disasters for both society and nature. In the midst of our headlong charge toward self-destruction, we would do well to turn to ancient values and their prophetic message for us today.

Throughout human history, yang-dominant culture and paradigms have oppressed yinish worldviews, limiting, if not outright eradicating, the necessary balancing function of yin. While the expansion of the patriarchal colonial powers took over the world, more feminine voices, such as those found in Taoism and Celtic spirituality, have been marginalized. There seems to be a correlation between the domination of nature and the domination of women. In fact, ecofeminists assert the interlocking dynamics between "historical, symbolic, and political relationships," and "the denigration of nature and the female."[8] Furthermore, they critique a disembodied worldview that separates the human from the cosmic and the mind from the body. Ecofeminism calls forth an alternative conceptual frame, one that reconnects body, nature, and cosmos, and thus promotes the holistic nature of the human being.

Ecofeminists' analysis of the modern worldview and plea for an alternative paradigm share an embodied worldview that parallels the yinist paradigm of Taoism and Celtic spirituality, moving from the inherently *disembodied* to a fuller, holistic, *embodied* worldview. The embodied paradigm of yinism requires the cessation of all extreme actions, including reckless development rooted in greed. In Taoism the concept of *Wuwei* functions as a representation of this radical cessation, a simple end to polluted and evil action.

---

8. Charlene Spetnak, "Critical and Constructive Contributions of Ecofeminism," in *Worldviews and Ecology: Religion, Philosophy, and the Environment*, ed. Mary Evelyn Tucker and John Grim (Philadelphia: Bucknell University Press, 1993), 181–89.

Wuwei: *Nonaction as Action*

One of the key concepts of Taoism is *Wuwei*, which may be translated as nonaction. It does not mean passivity but "a high standard or criterion, which means the most appropriate behavior. Wu (no) and wei (action) implies 'action as non-action.' In other words, *Wuwei* means 'actions with less risk or fewer side effects.' Practicing it requires great courage, confidence, and wisdom," writes Xiaogan.[9] Transforming our addiction to dizzying development requires nonaction prior to rash action. Often, solutions taken without the discipline of *Wuwei* ultimately exacerbate problems, fueling long-term destruction in order to facilitate short-term gains.

The Named and the Nameless Tao

Taoism is the only East Asian tradition that describes a differentiated confluence of the phenomenological world with the mysterious Ultimate Reality that lies beyond human language. In other words,

> Tao, the subtle reality of the universe cannot be described.
> That which can be described in words is merely a conception of the mind.
> Although names and descriptions have been applied to it,
> The subtle reality is beyond the description.[10]

Jung Young Lee, in his seminal book *The Trinity in Asian Perspective*, elucidates Lao Tzu's concept of unnameable ultimate reality:

> God transcends our knowing. God cannot be categorized in our finite expressions. Thus, in principle, The God who is told is not the real God. The Name that can be named is not

---

9. Liu Xiaogan, "Non-Action (*Wuwei*) and the Environment Today: A Conceptual and Applied Study of Laozi's Philosophy," in *Daoism and Ecology: Ways within a Cosmic Landscape*, ed. N. J. Girardot, James Miller, and Liu Xiaogan (Cambridge, MA: Harvard University Press, 2001).

10. Hua-Ching Ni, trans., *The Complete Works of Lao Tzu: Tao Teh Ching & Hua Hu Ching* (Santa Monica, CA: Seven Star Communications, 1993), 7.

the real Name. He illustrates God who said to Moses, "I am who I am" is the unnameable God, who transcends all the names we can attribute to God.[11]

Lao Tzu sees the transcendent, immanent, and post-Cartesian merging that is *Wuwei* (emptying one's mind of desire). Considering the fact that our own presuppositions determine what we see, it is crucial to empty ourselves of what we know if we are to see the nameless, the transcendent world. Likewise, there are many references to emptying in the Bible that relate to the road to conversion and transformation. Among many passages, I find Philippians 2 drawing a strong parallel between *Wuwei* and Jesus emptying himself (Philippians 2:7): "rather he made himself nothing" (NIV); "but emptied himself" (NRSV).

Triadic Structure of Primordial Energies

Chi-Tim Lai explains the concept of Central Harmony as the triadic structure of Primordial Energies, or qi (ch'i)— the great yang, the great yin, and the energy between them. The union of these three qi/ch'i and reciprocal communication are key ingredients of Central Harmony:

> Dao gave birth to the One. The One gave birth to the Two. The Two gave birth to the Three. And the Three gave birth to the ten thousand things. The ten thousand things carry yin on their backs and wrap their arms around yang. Through the blending of qi they arrive at a state of harmony.[12]

Conversely, cosmic disorder results from the lack of reciprocal communication, which disrupts the proper functioning of the yin and yang qi/ch'i. Mutual love and reciprocal communication

---

11. Lee, *The Trinity*, 12–13.

12. Chi-Tim Lai, "The Daoist Concept of Central Harmony in the Scripture of Great Peace: Human Responsibility for the Maladies of Nature," in *Daoism and Ecology: Ways within a Cosmic Landscape*, ed. N. J. Girardot, James Miller, and Liu Xiaogan (Cambridge, MA: Harvard University Press, 2001), 101.

between all three elements in the various structures of the cosmos will accompany Great Peace.

Similarly, pre-Christian Celtic culture was fascinated with triads and the number three, as in Taoism. Early Irish myth and art shows triads, trefoils (three-leaved plants), and triple figures. George Hunter writes:

> The Irish, perhaps from the teachings of the druids or the primal religion that preceded the druids, were aware that Ultimate Reality was mysterious and complex, and they were comfortable with paradox.[13]

Thus, the doctrine of the Trinity made an easy entry into Irish culture when St. Patrick introduced the gospel to the Celts. Jung Young Lee differentiates the two contrasting worldviews of the Western (substantive) and the Eastern (relational). He elaborates,

> When the Trinity is understood conceptually as substance or entity, it gives rise to contradictions resulting from the attempt to distinguish logically between one and three. However, when understood from the idea of change, three and one are not only interdependent but also inseparably related one to another as one in three and three in one.[14]

Therefore, yin-yang cosmology is trinitarian because it presupposes change as the ultimate reality. Lee thus sees the trinitarian principle as one of process. The ultimate reality is not static but dynamic, and demonstrates that "change is more fundamental than being."[15]

Celtic Worldviews

Contemporary postmodernism bears a striking resemblance to the premodern ancient traditions of Taoism and Celtic spiritu-

---

13. George G. Hunter III, *The Celtic Way of Evangelism: How Christianity Can Reach the West Again* (Nashville, TN: Abingdon Press, 2000), 81.

14. Lee, *The Trinity*, 66.

15. Ibid., 62.

ality. Upon a brief review of the divergent hermeneutical categories, I became fascinated by the fusion of the two horizons, Celtic and Taoist spirituality, that flourished in parallel during the fourth century BCE. Furthermore, as elaborated by J. Phillip Newell, the Celtic evangelism to the islands of Ireland and Britain exemplifies the weaving together of the gospel with the pre-Christian indigenous culture, the Druidic religion of nature mysticism. This was so seamlessly achieved as to result in not even a single martyr.

The early Irish and Scots felt that the Christianity brought by St. Columba and St. Patrick coalesced harmoniously with their pre-existing culture. Furthermore, the Celtic world, free from Greco-Roman culture, gave much more respect to the role of women and "more fully incorporated both the feminine and the masculine into religious life and imagery," asserts Newell.[16] Among evangelicals, Ralph Winter and George Hunter are also keen on Celtic Christianity, and they see crucial implications for our post-Christendom era. Implicitly, the Celtic worldview honored yin/yang harmony and shared the unity of the two, which the Celts also described as the Ultimate Reality.

The emphasis on seeing goodness and God as present within all that has life originates from both Druidic mysticism and respect for nature. Pelagius's panentheistic understanding of God as fluid not rigid, spiritual not doctrinal, and interweaving not dissecting offers a yinist perspective that balances yang-exclusive Cartesian theology. In the Western paradigm, Ludwig Wittgenstein also uses the same metaphor—"the flow of life"—introduced by Taoist scholar Chuang Tzu more than a millennium earlier.

Newell notes that one of the most pronounced marks of Celtic spirituality is highlighted by Pelagius's portrayal of "the elements of the earth as expressions of God's grace and goodness,"[17] as well as "our capacity to glimpse what [Pelagius] called 'the shafts

---

16. J. Phillip Newell, *Listening for the Heartbeat of God: A Celtic Spirituality* (New York: Paulist Press, 1997), 27–28.

17. Ibid., 5.

of divine light' that penetrate the thin veil dividing heaven and earth."[18]

Pelagius's understanding of the divine as unifying rather than separating God from God's creation corresponds to Lao Tzu's sense of ultimate reality. It is fascinating that Pelagius and Lao Tzu shared a similar cosmology that espouses the interweaving of heaven and earth, the visible and the invisible, and time and eternity. Both traditions see goodness in nature, while soberly acknowledging the danger of chaos. As early as the fourth and fifth centuries BCE both Taoism and Celtic spirituality, from which we have so much to learn, embraced respecting women.

An embrace of Thomas Cahill's description of Irish natural mysticism, which sees the whole as holy, would help our world to flourish rather than threaten the very sustainability of all living organisms:

> It was on this sturdy insight that Patrick choreographed the sacred dance of Irish sacramental life, a sacramentality not limited to the symbolic actions of the church's liturgy but open to the whole created universe. All the world was holy, and so was all the body.[19]

Contrary to Augustine's emphasis on original sin, Pelagius's anthropology was more balanced in the way he saw goodness without dismissing the reality of evil.

As Cahill notes, Celtic spirituality in the seventh century was rooted in John and emphasized "the practice of listening for the heartbeat of God" as the key to spirituality. In contrast, the Roman mission concentrated on the authority of Peter and thus argued for "a listening for God in the ordained teaching and life of the Church."[20] A synod of the church (664 CE) convened by Oswy, the king of North Umbria, decided to favor the Roman mission and pushed Celtic spirituality to the margins.

---

18. Ibid., 6.

19. Thomas Cahill, *How the Irish Saved Civilization: The Untold Story of Ireland's Heroic Role from the Fall of Rome to the Rise of Medieval Europe* (New York: Doubleday, 1995), 135.

20. Ibid., 1–2.

The primary distinction between Celtic and Roman spirituality lies in the fact that the Celtic mission and passion was to find God at the heart of all life—its emphasis was thus on creation. Contrary to Augustinian spirituality, which separates God from God's creation, the Celts recognized "the world as the place of revelation and the whole of life as sacramental."[21]

Newell also describes teaching that coincides with Taoism:

> Much of Pelagius' teaching can be seen to stem from the Wisdom tradition of the Old Testament. He saw Christ as the fulfillment of that tradition. Again, his Celtic emphasis was not so much on religious belief and the doctrines of the Church as on living a life of wisdom; by that he meant such things as loving all people, friends and enemies alike, and doing good in return for evil.[22]

As a woman, I feel compelled to highlight Pelagius's empowerment of women. This push toward empowerment regretfully drew persistent criticism from Augustine, who eventually labeled Pelagius a heretic. How different our church history would be if Pelagius's teaching were incorporated into mainstream theology, as complementary to Augustine's theology, which focused on original sin. Perhaps Christianity would have been less dogmatic and less damaging to our environment if Augustine had not rejected the teachings of Pelagius. As a yinist, my preference for Pelagius over Augustine is obvious.

A Yinist Paradigm: The Convergence of Taoism and Celtic Spirituality

The commonalities between Taoist and Celtic worldviews are striking. Figure 1 lists areas of overlap between these two ancient worldviews:

---

21. Ibid., 3.

22. Newell, *Listening for the Heartbeat*, 11. Celtic spirituality parallels Pelagius's theology (in contrast to Augustine's) in the sense that Pelagius does not divide Christianity from the rest of God's creation. On this point, Pelagius's cosmological spirituality contrasts with Augustine's dogmatic theology.

Taoist	Celtic
The nameless eternal Tao	Belief in ultimate reality
Interweaving of yin/yang	Interweaving of heaven and earth
Paradox	Paradox
Triad	Triad
Respect for women	Respect for women
Divine in nature	Divine in natural revelation
Analogies	Analogies
Monastery	Monastery
Aesthetic	Aesthetic
Mystic	Mystic
Wisdom	Wisdom
Communal	Communal
Tao Te Ching (embodied truth)	Embodied truth
Art	Art
Inner landscape	Inner landscape
Imagination	Imagination
Poetry	Poetry

Figure 1. Similarities of Taoist and Celtic worldviews

Most of the items listed in Figure 1 are yinist. Again, the concept of yinism is a duality, not dualism. Yinism does not seek to place yin in the foreground while relegating yang to the background. Instead, both are to coexist in balance and complementarity.

Through the right-brained faculty of imagination and the language of poetry, both Taoism and Celtic spirituality are revealed to be about embodied truth. The interweaving of human being, nature, and the Ultimate Reality flows like a kaleidoscopic movement. In fact, the Celts believed that poets mediated between heaven and earth. Such mysticism combined the "down to earth" (yin) with the "transcendent heaven" (yang), making both traditions appealing in our highly mechanistic world today.

The holistic, organic worldviews of Taoism and Celtic spirituality help us to overcome the dualism of "theology from above" and "theology from below." The close relationship between human beings and nature calls forth an important responsibility of human beings to take care of, not to have dominion over, God's creation. We can foster either Central Harmony or deterioration of the earth. The concept of Central Harmony in Taoism is a key to the health of all living organisms. Being a good steward of God's creation requires a worldview focused on the interdependence of human beings and nature so that we may maintain the harmonization of the organic process of nature, heaven, and earth. For this reason, I appreciate the holistic nature of ecofeminism in eschewing the oversimplified impulse to replace patriarchal reductionism with feminist reductionism.

All three traditions—Taoism, Celtic spirituality, and Christianity—affirm the Central Harmony that sustains all living organisms in the universe. As forewarned by the inherited guilt of Taoists, when human beings violate such mandates to our God-given nature, we end up accumulating evil, which reaps vicious cycles of disaster upon the earth.

Celtic, Taoist, and Christian traditions envisioned transcendent reality through the number three. Jung Young Lee views the Trinity from the tri-unifying aspect of Taoism, while Celtic scholars George G. Hunter, Thomas Cahill, Oliver Davies, Thomas O'Loughlin and others document the innate Celtic affinity for the Trinity.

Another noteworthy observation is the fact that both Taoist and Celtic worldviews imbue yin qualities in the foreground and yang in the background. Initially unassimilated to the yangish Roman imperial expansion, Celtic Christianity portrays the kaleidoscopic flow of life. Newell explains the Celtic gospel that was beautifully interwoven with the core of the Celtic ethos:

> When we look at a map of the Celtic lands even today we can see that their evangelization, begun in the fifth century, did not erase the marks of pre-Christian religion but rather transformed them, allowing some of the old stories and holy place-names and traditions to be woven into the fabric of the

gospel tradition. . . . The gospel was seen as fulfilling rather than destroying the old Celtic mythologies.[23]

Thomas Cahill stresses that Irish Christianity is "the first de-Romanized Christianity in human history, a Christianity without the sociopolitical baggage of the Greco-Roman world, a Christianity that completely acculturated itself into the Irish scene."[24]

Many insights can be drawn from the Irish example as we seek enculturation of an Asian American context into the evangelical theologies of the twenty-first century. As we face a world of extreme consumerism and environmental crisis, the shared worldviews of these two ancient traditions offer solace, hope, and a framework for moving forward. In the following section, I portray a yinist Jesus in John 4 to illustrate yinist theology in action through Jesus's encounter with the *alien Other* whom he transforms into *a residential host*.

Jesus Christ and a Yinist Praxis
for Theological Wholeness

Asian American Christianity often portrays a yinist Jesus—vulnerable, humble, merciful, loving, sacrificial, and steadfast. This image is in sharp contrast to a yangish vision of God as an omnipotent ruler and king. Reading the Gospel narratives of Jesus, particularly from John's Gospel, we can identify with a Jesus who exemplifies the values of Taoism, Celtic spirituality, and yinism. We see this exemplification demonstrated through Jesus's reversal of the cultural concept of power through his vulnerability, sacrifice, acceptance, and love. Jesus's encounter with the Samaritan woman at the well brings wholeness to a broken woman. His approach here is likened to a yinist praxis of fusion, unification, and holistic relating. Likewise, Asian American evangelicals yearn for such an encounter with first-generation Christian leaders.

---

23. Newell, *Listening for the Heartbeat*, 27.
24. Cahill, *How the Irish Saved Civilization*, 148.

The Power of Vulnerability

Jesus's curriculum is both open and contextual. His teaching, therefore, takes place in the synagogues, fields, homes, and even at the well, when he is exhausted and in need of a drink. As he sat down by the well, a Samaritan woman came to draw water, thinking that no one else was around. From a position of weakness, without a bucket, Jesus approaches the woman and asks her for a drink (John 4:6–7). Jesus did not preface this conversation with either a formal greeting or with small talk. Without any misgivings, he immediately, and quite earnestly, treats her as someone who could simply help him quench his thirst. After all, she came to draw water. This simple act of asking for a drink, however, is significantly multifaceted and transcends all human prejudices. By asking a favor from a Samaritan woman, Jesus redefined who she truly is and can be. He repositioned her from her disposition.

Of great relevance for theological education today is the vulnerability of Jesus. It is not the mighty who thaw the icy walls of gender, race, class, and religion. It is through the vulnerability of weakness. Too frequently, empowerment is imposed from the top to the bottom. This structure serves only to perpetuate a vicious circle of injustice.

Theological education today is in need of both sharpening and softening its power through vulnerable service to humanity in crisis. Seminarians, reflecting the macropopulation, are broken and hungry for wholeness. Jesus affirmed and challenged the Samaritan woman, and she became whole. People today thirst for such an encounter.

A startling irony is that the very encounter seminarians hunger for lies beyond the reach of the institutions of which they are a part. Theological education should move toward encountering deeper stages of knowledge and awareness, even questioning its deep-seated orthodoxy. For such an engagement to be possible, theological waters need to be reexamined and revised. It demands the plunge into an intimate transforming process as demonstrated by the woman who rediscovered herself and thus discovered her life's mission.

True spirituality sends us down a road toward truth—wherever that may lead. In the words of Parker Palmer, "It will understand that fear, not ignorance, is the enemy of learning, and that fear is what gives ignorance its power. It will try to root out our fear of having our ignorance exposed and our orthodoxies challenged."[25] The road to educational renewal demands a willingness to be remolded like clay in the potter's hands. It demands a turn from mere intellectual rigor and a return to its integration of interior and communal processes.

The sad reality today is that educational values and their praxis favor monologue rather than dialogue, thus maintaining the status quo. Even when the importance of dialogue is introduced, it is done via monologue. In a one-sided educational setting, a communal encounter between the teacher and learner, and between learner and learner, is not feasible.

Yinist theology identifies with Jesus Christ, the migrant God of simplicity, who is vulnerable, humble, loving, compassionate, and peaceful. The emerging Asian American generation seeks this kind of authenticity. They hope and long for the kind of true and genuine community Jesus formed wherever he went. From my work with Asian Americans of the emerging generation, I hear their yearning for meaningful relationships with the preceding generations and an authentic encounter with Jesus Christ, as the Samaritan woman experienced.

Asian American Evangelical Christianity

Compared to the 1990s, today's Asian American seminary enrollment has rapidly diminished. Still echoing in my ears is the outcry of the Asian American seminarians for mentors during the '90s when there were large numbers who committed themselves to ministry through church camps and parachurch influence on college campuses:

---

25. Parker Palmer, *To Know as We Are Known: Education as a Spiritual Journey* (San Francisco: HarperSanFrancisco, 1993), xi.

greater Asian American consciousness is the growing evangelical, charismatic, and Pentecostal presence within and
independent of Catholicism and mainline Protestant denominations. Evangelical Asian Americans are predominantly Second Wave immigrants and their children.[26]

In his 1997 research, Donald Miller refers to second-wave Asian
American congregations as "new paradigm churches," whose
leadership equates consumer marketing with evangelical church
growth. Consequently, "Asian American consciousness" is reduced
into a marketing strategy, overlooking the Asian American experiences of racism. This otherworldly theology leaves ample room for
this world to be hijacked by the corporate value of *maximum profit
of the few*, which has brutally increased the income gap between
the rich and the poor while chipping away at the middle class. We
can also testify to how such an ideology impacts the very environment we rely on for our sustainability.

The main mission of Asian American evangelical churches tends
to reflect conservative evangelicalism, focusing on proclamation,
church growth, church planting, and charity. For example, the
mainstream's core agendas of human sexuality, gender equality,
and poverty issues appear to be overlooked by middle-class Asian
American churches. Thus far, the spiritual vitality of the first-
generation immigrant church was in providing immigrants with a
home away from home. Adjusting to life in the new land is an ardu-
ous undertaking. This community of believers serves to mitigate
myriad challenges: linguistic, social, and cultural. It is no small
accomplishment that the Asian American immigrant church has
managed to shrink the barriers of access to American life for their
generation and for generations to come.

26. Timothy Tseng et al., *Pulpit and Pew Research on Pastoral Leadership: Asian American Religious Leadership Today: A Preliminary Inquiry*
(Durham, NC: Duke Divinity School, 2005), 15.

Attraction to Charismatic Christianity

Non-Western culture lacks an innate affinity with what Paul Hiebert calls a two-tiered Platonic dualism of this world and the other world. This dualism excludes the middle zone, therefore marginalizing meaning that is expressed through the guidance of ancestor spirits, angels, and folktales. The Western Christian mission, with its two-tiered worldview, eliminates the middle zone by calling it superstition without offering a Christian substitution. In response to pressure, the middle zone is submerged but does not disappear.

For example, Paul Yongi Cho provided major leadership in filling the excluded middle zone through healing, fasting, and all-night prayer meetings. In doing so, he touched the core of the Korean ethos, an ethos that could not have been met by rational Western Christianity. It was one of the most acculturated forms of Protestant spirituality in Korea. It is noteworthy that second-generation Korean Americans also yearn for such a primal connection.

During a roundtable session with second-generation Korean American seminarians at Fuller Seminary, I learned how much the current generation longs for an authentic relationship with church leadership, particularly with first-generation leaders. All eleven students, both male and female, poured out their longing in their struggle with the "neither/nor" identity of nonbelongingness. They described the Korean first-generation culture as *performance-oriented* and *result-oriented*, with only numerical measurements for success (yang). Meanwhile, American culture was seen as more *process-oriented* (yin). On the other hand, when they differentiated Korean spirituality from its American counterpart, the yin/yang traits were reversed. Korean spirituality centered on the heart and on fervency (yin) and the American on the head (yang). One female Korean American seminarian said,

> The Korean sense of spirituality is so passionate with foolish longing. I often long for shouting, Joo Yeo (Please, Oh Lord!), but the English translation does not carry the deeper meaning. I have a hunger for Korean fervent prayer that connects

us with our common narratives. The independent English-speaking congregations are like orphaned churches with no parents, no grandparents; they lack wisdom.[27]

Another female student shared the same view about Korean spirituality and critiqued the mainstream Presbyterian Church USA as a head without a heart, as she explained why she left PC USA for a charismatic church. To her, "head without heart" is meaningless. "I learned a lot about budgets, doctrine, commissioning," she said. "But we want a real God. We don't want God encased in books."

One male student described how building projects for sanctuaries and gymnasiums are meaningless when building future leaders is neglected. "We want authentic community," he said. "We haven't been empowered to be adults."

Another youth pastor shared his frustration with his head pastor: "My pastor doesn't care about youth, and he considers youth ministry to be advanced babysitting."

The current emerging generation's pursuit of God is not yang-ish (masculine energy). They are not focused on an omnipotent, almighty, *the-bigger-the-better* version of Christianity. Instead they gravitate for a yinish (feminine energy) spirituality—one with a nurturing and integrative God. Notably, second-generation Korean Americans seem to reject the church as a family based on Confucian values and, instead, seek a nonhierarchical, authentic community. According to them, our deeply embedded Confucianism needs to be reexamined in light of biblical teaching.

In the end, the roundtable participants synthesized a triad of values for their faith moving forward: Korean fervent spirituality rooted in communal prayer, American spirituality of social justice and process, and biblical truth. For such a yin/yang dialectical synthesis to take place, ongoing intergenerational listening sessions are required. The second generation's longing for an intergenerational

---

27. A Korean American female seminarian shared her observations on the uniqueness of Korean Christianity during a roundtable listening session at Fuller Theological Seminary, as part of the National Council of Korean Presbyterian Church USA, on October 24, 2005.

reciprocal relationship and mutual respect is embodied in Jesus, who presented himself both as a guest and a host at the well. The hunger for nurturance is also modeled beautifully by Jesus as most of his teaching took place by simply spending time with his disciples in daily life.

A Time for *Wuwei*

The first generation's relentless work ethic, coupled with spiritual fervency, total loyalty, and sacrifice to ministry, leaves little room for family time or recuperation from ministry. The need for a regular sabbatical, temporary withdrawal from ministry would provide renewal and thus sustain pastors in ministry, avoiding burnout and the tragic exit from ministry all together. To enact a widespread practice of sustainable ministry would require the transformation of not only our philosophy of ministry but also theology itself. The exclusion of yinist spirituality in fact plagues the very numerical success of some first-generation megachurches today because they do not care for a yinish interior landscape.

Our emerging generation's level of frustration with the Confucian hierarchy of their parents' generation also depicts their love for and connection with their roots. While seeking to move beyond the confines of the Korean American church toward multicultural and pan-Asian American churches, they continue to identify with the first generation's spirituality and spiritual discipline. Hunger for intergenerational bonding, prior to moving beyond Korean ethnic churches, was strong among the roundtable participants. I was deeply moved by the level of sharing that took place. The yearning for dialogue, understanding, and mature self-critique permeated the roundtable fellowship. As keenly aware as they are of the harmful imbalance of exclusively yang culture from both the Korean Confucian hierarchy and corporate American and global culture, the emerging generation seeks the balancing of yin and yang that reconciles, renews, and thus exudes health in the body of Christ.

Staring at the vacuum of the middle zone, the younger Asian American generations are attracted to the charismatic expression of faith, thus leaving the more cerebral focus of mainline denominations. This is why constructing Asian American evangelical theologies is crucial. Creating an Asian American evangelical hermeneutical circle will serve to fill our current theological vacuum, which abandons Asian American pastors to simply shop for the latest fads in ministry models, offering quick, and often superficial, results.

What would it take for Asian American churches to be empowered enough to see ourselves as a hermeneutical circle? It would take brutally honest dialogue among Asian American scholars and pastoral leaders, as exemplified in Jesus's encounter with the Samaritan woman. Only such open dialogue will provide the opportunity for the legacies of the hard-working, first-generation ministry to be transmitted to the younger generation. The alternative is a continuation of the current cycle of nontransmission, which results in each new generation being burdened with having to develop from scratch knowledge, practice, and the deeper elements of spirit and relationship. To advance this new vision, I offer a yinist theological paradigm for an Asian American theology that is holistic, Asian, Celtic, and evangelical, extending good news to all God's creation.

An internalized theological paternalism, one that excludes innate Asianness while putting forward the two-tiered Cartesian paradigm, cannot sustain our emerging generation today. These models have left us with personal and cultural wounds that are evidenced in our low ministerial retention rates. New wineskin must be offered for new wine. For this, I have attempted to construct a holistic Christian theology, yinist, utilizing the convergent worldviews of Taoism and Celtic spirituality.

• 3 •

Spirituality and Ecology

As our ecosystem radically changes, we witness a dramatic human toll due to extreme floods, droughts, and massive oil spills. Meanwhile, politicians remain stuck in endless ideological debates, and some even continue to oppose the science behind global climate change, in effect denying our dire environmental situation. Modernity disconnected humanity from the rest of God's creation, and the evangelical Christian faith increasingly upholds and furthers this position.[1] As a result, too many of us stand idly by as we witness the poisoning and squandering of our most basic resources: the air we breathe and the water we drink. Daily reports come in of catastrophic air pollution, scarce access to clean water, rising ocean levels that fuel hurricanes, record snow in the northeastern United States, and severe droughts on the West Coast. In California, farmers lack water to produce their crops while many residents insist on watering decorative lawns. The *Los Angeles Times* runs stories about the hopeless decline of Antarctic glaciers, and droves of disaster reports numb us as we experience "the groaning of all creation" (Romans 8:22).[2]

My journey toward ecological living began in 1992 with the study and understanding of the Asian cosmology of Taoism. Impacted by

---

1. See, for example, Andrew Spencer, "Three Reasons Why Evangelicals Stopped Advocating for the Environment," *Christianity Today* (June 14, 2017), https://www.christianitytoday.com.

2. Scott Gold, "Irreversible Collapse of Antarctic Glaciers Has Begun, Studies Say," *Los Angeles Times*, May 12, 2014, http://www.latimes.com.

internalized syncretism, I could not initially embrace Taoism as a theological paradigm. But once I encountered Austrian American physicist Fritjof Capra's seminal book *The Tao of Physics*, I felt free to investigate a Taoist cosmology.

For Capra, Taoism provided an explanation for the both/and phenomenon in quantum physics. In turn, Taoism also provided an alternative paradigm to my dissonance with the reductionist Cartesian paradigm found in educational curricula. Emboldened by the connection between quantum physics and Taoism and compelled to contribute a voice for Asian American feminism to the conversation, I found that my yinist concept could fill a long-standing void. Unfortunately, the presentation of the yinist paradigm has been a lonely journey. Fellow Christians too often marginalize the idea as either too foreign to the dominant discourse or as hopelessly syncretistic.

The Fear of Syncretism

Despite Christianity's long-standing history of Judaization, Hellenization, Westernization, and others, a persistent fear of syncretism remains a stumbling block in approaching Christianity through cultural lenses. As German theologian Adolf von Harnack puts it, "From the very outset [Christianity] had been syncretistic upon pagan soil; it made its appearance, not as a gospel pure and simple, but equipped with all that Judaism had already acquired during the course of its long history."[3] Additionally, missiologist Lamin Sanneh states, "Pluralism was rooted for Paul in the Gentile experience, which in turn justified intercultural openness in mission. . . . As the absolute gift of a loving, gracious God, faith is the leveling, transcendent force in culture."[4]

---

3. Adolf von Harnack, *The Mission and Expansion of Christianity in the First Three Centuries*, vol. 1 (New York: Putnam, 1908), 314, quoted in Lamin Sanneh, *Translating the Message: The Missionary Impact on Culture*, American Society of Missiology Series 42, 2nd ed. (Maryknoll, NY: Orbis Books, 2009), 49.

4. Ibid., 54.

The yinist paradigm faces the obstacle of a general lack of familiarity among Americans. Even among Asian Americans educated in
the United States, there is very little exposure to innate Asian concepts such as Taoism. Yet Taoism speaks to all areas of life, from
ecology to diet. Its ancient, comprehensive cosmology is as relevant
today as ever, especially as Mother Earth moans and groans under
the weight of seven billion inhabitants.

This chapter first explores the origins of the Protestant disconnect between humanity and God on the one hand and humanity
and the rest of God's creation on the other. Second, I will interact with convergent theologies: Yinist cosmology with both ecotheology and planetary theology. These three systems share similar
concerns and strive to retrieve the lost concept of ecological stewardship—humanity's responsibility as caretakers, not conquerors,
of God's creation.

N. J. Girardot, James Miller, and Liu Xiaogan's *Daoism and
Ecology* addresses pertinent questions regarding the role of religion
and ecology:

1. Have issues of personal salvation superseded all others?
2. Have divine/human relations been primary?
3. Have anthropocentric ethics been all-consuming?
4. Has the material world of nature been devalued by religion?
5. Does the search for otherworldly rewards override commit-
   ment to this world?
6. Did religions simply surrender their natural theologies and
   concerns with exploring purpose in nature to positivistic scientific cosmologies?[5]

The answer to these questions continues to be "yes," calling for an
investigation of the historical roots of this regrettable divorce from
the concept of ecological stewardship.

5. N. J. Girardot, James Miller, and Liu Xiaogan, eds., *Daoism and Ecology: Ways within a Cosmic Landscape* (Cambridge, MA: Harvard University
Press, 2001), xvii.

The Historical Roots of the Desacralization of Nature

The key architects of modernity elevated humanity while reducing nature to a subjugated and utilitarian role. This was a critical departure from the medieval view of nature as sacred and mystical. Among these modernist thinkers are Thomas Hobbes, René Descartes, and Bertrand Russell. Hobbes "audaciously desacralized and demystified the medieval view of nature."[6] Descartes took Hobbes's view further and saw humans as "lords and possessors of nature."[7] And Russell posited that "God might have made the world, but that is no reason why we should not make it over."[8]

Perhaps more than any other person, Francis Bacon ushered in the reductionistic and mechanistic worldviews of modernity, promulgating the subjugation of nature. Bacon focused on the practical pursuit of scientific knowledge and technological innovation, relating it to biblical and religious ideas more congenial to Protestant England.[9] Hence, Bacon's work began the era of early modern scientific enterprise that ignited the manipulation of nature for human purposes. Departing from the patristic and medieval reverence toward nature, this seventeenth-century scientific paradigm became a dominant force, utilizing Greek philosophy in the subjugation of nature while also claiming these anthropocentric ideas to be "biblical."[10] The theology of dominion, rooted in the literal interpretation of the Genesis texts, then bolstered this secularized view of nature.

---

6. Douglas J. Hall, "Stewardship as Key to a Theology of Nature," in *Environmental Stewardship: Critical Perspectives—Past and Present*, ed. R. J. Berry (London: T&T Clark International, 2006), 132–33.

7. Nicols Fox, *Against the Machine: The Hidden Luddite Tradition in Literature, Art and Individual Lives* (Washington, DC: A Shearwater Book, Island Press, 2002), 298.

8. Bertrand Russell, *The Scientific Outlook* (New York: Routledge, 2009), 108.

9. Richard Bauckham, "Modern Domination of Nature: Historical Origins and Biblical Critique," in *Environmental Stewardship: Critical Perspectives—Past and Present*, ed. R. J. Berry (London: T&T Clark International, 2006), 39–40.

10. Ibid., 33.

Drawing from Genesis 1:28, Bacon connected the idea of human capacity to reshape the world at will with God-given human dominion over nature, a dominion that had been impaired by the fall of Adam and Eve. Therefore, he envisioned the recovery of this dominion through "the technological exploitation of nature for human benefit."[11] Today, this seventeenth-century worldview continues to dictate contemporary theological disconnection with nature. The history of these philosophical underpinnings offers clarification and possible solutions. In the mid-twentieth century, historian Lynn White Jr. traced the ecological crisis to the Hebraic-Christian religion rooted in Greek philosophical tradition that bifurcates the sacred as otherworldly and the profane as worldly, writing that "Man and nature are two things, and man is master."[12] A polemical worldview justifies the biblical concept of dominion in Genesis 1:28. *Kabash* (subdue) comes from a Hebrew root meaning "to tread down," which conveys the image of a heavy-footed man.[13] The connotation of *radah* (dominion) also conveys "treading" or "trampling" and suggests the image of a conqueror. The table below lists the contrast between the Hebrew and Greek worldviews. Concerned scholars lament the misuse and justification of Genesis 1:28 with little sense of responsibility for the stewardship of God's creation.[14]

The Hebrew and Greek Worldviews

As the chart below demonstrates,[15] core shapers of Christianity stem from Hebrew and Hellenic cultures:

---

11. Ibid., 37.

12. Lynn White Jr., "The Historical Roots of Our Ecologic Crisis," *Science* 155, no. 3767 (March 10, 1967): 1203–7, at 1205.

13. Loren Wilkinson, "Global Housekeeping: Lords or Servants?" *Christianity Today*, July 24, 1980, 27.

14. Ross Kinsler and Gloria Kinsler, *The Biblical Jubilee and the Struggle for Life: An Invitation to Personal, Ecclesial, and Social Transformation* (Maryknoll, NY: Orbis Books, 1999), 25.

15. John Zizioulas, "Priest of Creation," in *Environmental Stewardship: Critical Perspectives—Past and Present*, ed. R. J. Berry (London: T&T Clark International, 2006), 275–76.

Hebrew Worldview	Greek Worldview
Emphasized importance of history	Deemphasized importance of history
God reveals Godself mainly in history	Viewed history with distrust
Nature played a secondary role in this revelation	Nature was viewed as a source of security
Book of Revelation: "cosmological prophecy"	Cosmology was a major concern of the Greek philosophers
Rising above history: marks the beginning of a new approach to human relationship with nature	Saw God present and operating in and through its laws of cyclical movement and natural reproduction

As shown in the chart above, the Hebrews emphasized history over cosmology. The Greeks, however, were suspicious of history and instead regarded nature as the source of security. Hence, for the Greeks, cosmology was a matter of concern, and they saw God's presence in the cyclical movement of nature.[16] This view is similar to the Taoist worldview.

The introduction of Gnosticism, however, engendered a view of the material world in opposition to the nonmaterial world. And with the belief that the *imago Dei* was tethered to human consciousness and introspection, the superiority of humanity over nature became the dominant view. The early church embraced the negative attitudes of Gnosticism, despite opposition from key leaders such as Irenaeus, the bishop of Lyons. Nature also had no place in Augustine's theology; the eternal soul was his main concern. Nature all but disappeared from sacramental theology in the West.

Scholasticism and the Reformation also associated the *imago*

---

16. Ibid., 275.

Dei with human reason, widening the gap between humanity and nature. The Enlightenment extended the divide even more until only rational being mattered. Furthermore, Romanticism solidified the dichotomy between the thinking, conscious subject and non-thinking, nonconscious nature. Pietism, mysticism, and other traditions also separated their theologies from nature. Puritanism and mainstream Calvinism justified the absence of nature in theology through decontextualized verses in Genesis compelling humanity "to multiply and to dominate the earth." This gave "rise to capitalism and eventually to the technology"[17] that today dominates Western civilization. Max Weber posited that the Protestant ethic's separation from nature fostered the spirit of capitalism and vice versa. Calvinists, more than any other denomination, took profit and material success as signs of God's favor. The confluence of capitalism and Calvinism unleashed the spirit of modern capitalism, which then took on a life of its own.[18]

In summary, the lineage of the polemic worldview can be traced through Gnosticism, scholasticism, Darwinism, the Reformation, the Enlightenment, Romanticism, pietism, mysticism, puritanism, Calvinism, and the technological revolution. These all led to the dominance of a Western civilization with an anthropocentric, reason-dominated worldview.

The Modern Theological Worldview

The rise of modernity and Protestantism accompanied the desacralization of nature and thus shifted the worldview from the theocentric community of creation to an anthropocentric hierarchy. In fact, the anthropocentric view claims that it is humanity's duty and right to rule over the rest of God's creation, despite the fact that the Genesis creation narrative is theocentric, not anthropocentric. In his critique, theologian Douglas J. Hall raises pertinent questions for mission theology today:

17. Ibid.
18. Max Weber, *The Protestant Ethic and the Spirit of Capitalism* (New York: Routledge, 2009).

How can we reconcile (or can we?) the apparent contradictions of a religion that on the one hand clearly makes the world—God's good creation—the very object of the divine agape, and on the other hand seems to give to greedy anthropos all the justification needed for turning the beautiful place God made into a pigsty?[19]

With all of the conveniences modernity offers, the limitless valuing of "the bigger the better" finally confronts us with a dire flipside: the risk of destroying all of creation. Mother Nature is striking back with severe drought, tsunamis, and floods, endangering the very sustainability of earth's inhabitants.

The anthropocentric domination of nature has become the towering force of our time, sanctioned by modernity and its theology, combined with ubiquitous marketdom. French philosopher Jacques Ellul warns of the dangers society faces when we replace humanity with the machine. Ellul differentiates the external machine from internal technique. This technique, "the totality of methods rationally arrived at, and having absolute efficiency (for a given stage of development) involves every field of human activity."[20] Ellul's warning against the inevitable absorption of humanity by autonomous technique is becoming a reality today as robots increasingly replace humans in the workforce.

Framing the world solely as a resource for economic development accompanies the downward spiral of ecological degradation, social alienation, and violence. Ellul's seven characteristics of the technological society merit our attention today: (1) rationality, (2) artificiality, (3) automatism of technical choice, (4) self-augmentation, (5) monism, (6) technical universalism, and (7) autonomy. For Ellul, the dilemma all living organisms confront under modern civilization is the convergent forces of the "science-technology-commodity complex" that shapes and conditions humanity. The fusion of technology with capital demands endless technological

---

19. Hall, "Stewardship as Key," 132.
20. Jacques Ellul, *The Technological Society* (New York: Vantage Books, 1964), xxv.

innovation directed at the global market.[21] It also requires an insatiable demand for growth and profit.

In contrast, the medieval theology of stewardship viewed the earth as sacred and thus placed limits on how much of the earth humans could take. The loss of these previous traditions robbed humanity of restraint in the excessive use of the earth's resources. Anthropocentrism filled this vacuum, defining nature as godless and conveniently desacralizing nature for maximum human benefit and exploitation. The disconnection of humanity from the rest of God's creation therefore shifted theology from a question of stewardship to one of domination. Surely, humanity's unfettered industrial and technological advances, despite certain human benefits, have come at a steep cost for our planet.

Counterstream to Modernity

As Enlightenment logocentrism and humanism championed the anthropocentric worldview, key Romantics critiqued Cartesian reductionism: Giambattista Vico, Johann Gottfried Herder, Joseph De Maistre, and Johann Georg Hamann.[22] In speaking out against the reduction of irreducible realities, I resonate with their counter-Enlightenment critique of the "Cartesian fallacy." These Romantic critics foresaw a future where compartmentalized and fragmented realities would lead to the loss of meaning. Along with this sense of meaninglessness would come depression, anxiety, and violence against humanity and nature. An earlier countervoice from the West is the fourth-century moralist Pelagius, whose theology is expansively inclusive of all of God's creation. In contrast with his opponents, he emphasized the goodness of God's creation as a reflection of God rather than as separate from God's creation.[23]

---

21. José Luis Garcia, Helena Mateus Jerónimo, and Carl Mitcham, eds., *Jacques Ellul and the Technological Society in the 21st Century* (New York: Springer, 2013), 4.

22. Isaiah Berlin, *Three Critics of the Enlightenment: Vico, Hamann, Herder*, ed. Henry Hardy (Princeton, NJ: Princeton University Press, 2000).

23. J. Phillip Newell, *Listening for the Heartbeat of God: A Celtic Spirituality* (New York: Paulist Press, 1977), 13.

It is important to note that modernity is not entirely negative. On the contrary, developments in technology and science have improved human life enormously. However, all good things taken to their extremes result in imbalance. Managerial ecclesiology and numerically driven succession weaken the church's prophetic witness in the public sector.

The following section depicts my theological imagination—an attempt to construct a cosmocentric theology that departs from the anthropocentric approach to the Bible, God, and the world.

Theology of the Earth

The human-centered scientific worldview and the literal interpretation of Genesis texts contribute to the exploitation of land, sea, and sky. Historian Howard Snyder refers to this disconnect as "the great divorce of heaven and earth in Christian theology":

> The disease of sin brought alienation, a divorce between people, and their maker, and between people and their world, their habitat, which is planet earth. . . . Divorce IS an apt metaphor for the whole problem of the relationship between God, humans, and the earth.[24]

In bridging this "great divorce," Snyder emphasizes creation stewardship. Meanwhile German theologian Jürgen Moltmann emphasizes a trinitarian theology as foundational for stewardship. For Moltmann, trinitarian theology extends God's presence in God's creation through the unity of Father, Son, and Holy Spirit. This calls for a shift from a modern paradigm of domination to an alternative paradigm that links God, humanity, and earth. In the mid-1980s, Moltmann's Gifford Lectures at Edinburgh described the "ecological crisis" as a crisis of human domination over nature and of our understanding of God. Moltmann warned against seeing the world as godless and the sanctioning of humanity's destruc-

---

24. Howard Snyder, with Joe Scandrett, *Salvation Means Creation Healed: The Ecology of Sin and Grace. Overcoming the Divorce between Earth and Heaven* (Eugene, OR: Cascade Books, 2011), 3.

tive domination and exploitation of nature.[25] This theological disconnect bears substantial responsibility for our current ecological crisis. How can we shift our warped worldview and overcome the anthropocentrism that led to our current ecological crisis?

Often, the answers to problems exist within the problems themselves. If the bulk of the ecological crisis resides in a fragmented theological belief, then a reconnecting of the missing links in theological constructs offers an alternative paradigm. If the confluence of capitalism and Protestantism wreak havoc on the ecosystem, then recovering the abandoned theology of stewardship may curtail the excessively anthropocentric view of God's creation. Theoretical physicist Albert Einstein broke through the modern paradigm and began the postmodern paradigm of the unity between the observer and the observed. In response to the discoveries of quantum physics, the reign of the modern paradigm separating subject from object began to wane. Hence, postmodern holism emerged as a countervoice that sees reality as interrelated.

A Yinist Stewardship

I now propose a yinist epistemology, which partially parallels planetary theology and ecotheology. The yinist concept highlights yin, the Taoist feminine energy, over our current state of excessively dominant, masculine yang energy. Together, yin/yang is an inclusively interwoven both/and concept rather than an either/or concept. Overarching problems ensue with an imbalance of these two energies. Chinese medicine describes this imbalance in people as well as in ecosystems as disease. As a philosophical paradigm, Taoism promotes a balanced and holistic practice of simple living and responsible stewardship.

Placing yin explicitly in the foreground, the overburdened yang energy oscillates into the background. Rather than asserting and competing, the yin energy embraces and balances, encompassing

---

25. Jürgen Moltmann, *God in Creation: A New Theology of Creation and the Spirit of God,* The Gifford Lectures 1984–1985 (Minneapolis, MN: Fortress Press, 1993).

gender, ecology, nature, health, and God. Yin is holistic, synthesizing, and complementary. Yinist feminism, therefore, diffuses false dichotomies derived from dualistic paradigms: male versus female, humanity versus nature, God apart from humanity, this world apart from the other world.[26]

According to Jung Young Lee, the yin/yang concept offers a "cosmocentric anthropology" that comprehensively covers gender, nature, and food, among other things. Hence, according to Taoism, human beings and nature are inseparable. As noted in chapter 2, Lee's use of a Taoist lens to critique reductionistic Western theology greatly furthered the development of theology based on Asian paradigms.[27]

Tao is translated into English as "path" or "way"—the source of all living creatures.[28] The *Tao Te Ching*, which refers to the immanence and transcendence of formlessness and namelessness, was translated into Latin in the sixteenth century by Jesuit missionaries in China, and then presented by James Legge to the British Royal Society. The translators commented that the *Tao Te Ching* showed that "the Mysteries of the Most Holy Trinity and of the Incarnate God were anciently known to the Chinese nation."[29] In earlier research, I noted the confluent worldviews of Taoism and Celtic druids, which suggests the interchange of the two cultures (see Figure 1 in chapter 2).

In contrast to the yang-dominated Newtonian and Cartesian worldviews, Taoist and Celtic worldviews reflect both yin and

---

26. Young Lee Hertig, "The Asian American Alternative to Feminism: A Yinist Paradigm," *Missiology: Mission and Marginalization* 26, no. 1 (1998): 15–22.

27. Jung Young Lee, *The Trinity in Asian Perspective* (Nashville, TN: Abingdon Press, 1996), 18.

28. Paul S. Chung, "The Mystery of God and Dao in Jewish-Christian-Daoist Context," in *Asian Contextual Theology for the Third Millennium: Theology of Minjung in Fourth-Eye Formation*, ed. Paul S. Chung, Veli-Matti Kärkkäinen, and Kim Kyoung-Jae (Eugene, OR: Wipf & Stock, 2007), 245.

29. James Legge, *The Texts of Daoism,* vol. 1 (New York: Dover, 1962), xiii.

yang traits. The beauty of Taoism is its comprehensive approach to gender, ecology, nature, health, and food. Humanity and nature are inseparable in Taoism from the life-giving energy of ch'i extending to all creation. Ch'i keeps yin–yang from collapsing into dichotomy.[30]

Ruach and Ch'i

Overlaps between Taoist and Celtic spirituality correspond to overlaps between the Hebrew concept of *ruach* and the ancient Chinese cosmology of ch'i, and many Asian American theologians have researched the intersection of these concepts. Renewed interest in a pneumatological approach to theology, unlike the christological perspective, may steer these discourses in a unifying manner among world religions with "the ubiquity of the cosmic Spirit."[31]

Among theologians, Jürgen Moltmann from Germany and Stanley Samartha from India bridge Western and Eastern theology through the ubiquitous Spirit of *ruach*. As Koo Yun observes, Moltmann's pneumatologies and Taoists' ch'i connect the sacred Holy Spirit (the primordial ch'i) and the human spirit (substantial ch'i).[32]

Ch'i is the life force that interpenetrates all entities, animate and inanimate. Likewise, *ruach* is described by Yun as "a storm or force in both body and soul" that is found in everything, keeping all things in being and in life, similar to ch'i.[33] I concur with Yun's critique of Barthian theology's disconnection of God's Spirit from human spirit. A more convincing and helpful position is Moltmann's argument for the continuity of the Spirit in both God's creation and the church. Because of the fear of syncretism embedded

---

30. Chung, "The Mystery of God," 265.

31. Koo D. Yun, "Pneumatological Perspectives on World Religions: The Cosmic Spirit and Ch'i," in *Asian Contextual Theology for the Third Millennium: Theology of Minjung in Fourth-Eye Formation*, ed. Paul S. Chung, Veli-Matti Kärkkäinen, and Kim Kyoung-Jae (Eugene, OR: Wipf & Stock, 2007), 165.

32. Ibid., 168.

33. Ibid.

in many non-Western Christians, Moltmann's voice offers permission for Asian/Asian American theologians to bridge pneumatology and Taoism. They may offer a paradigmatic shift in our views of humanity, nature, God, and the Bible toward a more sustainable world.

(Yinist) Theology of the Heart

In the letter to the Romans, the apostle Paul emphasizes, "God's love has been poured into our hearts through the Holy Spirit that has been given to us" (5:5). And Luke states, "The good person out of the good treasure of the heart produces good" (Luke 6:45). A pioneer of Asian theology, Choan-Seng Song, echoes Scripture, stating, "To know one's heart is to know one's whole being."[34] Quoting prophets in the Hebrew Bible and the apostle Paul in the New Testament, Song emphasizes the importance of the integrated heart in a Western, reason-based theology and notes that the prophets Jeremiah and Ezekiel "highlight the conversion of the heart as most fundamental in our life."[35] The prophet Ezekiel speaks to the condition of a new heart: "I will give you a new heart and put a new spirit in you; I will remove from you your *heart of stone and give you a heart of flesh*" (36:26, italics added). Song interprets the two contrasting hearts: the former represents the heart in "revolt against God," and the latter as "the person who has been transformed by the redeeming love of God."[36]

The central theory in the school of Neo-Confucianism (e.g., Wang Yang Ming) is "the heart principle," which emphasizes cultivating the nature of the heart. The core Confucian principle of *li*, the essence of morality, integrates human experience with immanent transcendence. Neo-Confucianism synthesized Buddhism and Taoism with its principle of the heart. As a holistic theological construction, these principles emphasize the fact that the heart

---

34. Choan-Seng Song, *Third-Eye Theology: Theology in Formation in Asian Settings*, rev. ed. (Maryknoll, NY: Orbis Books, 1991), 71–72.

35. Ibid., 72.

36. Ibid.

embodies the whole person in relationship to God. A theology of heart cultivates human hearts, creating a bridge to the reductionistic Cartesian theology of the West. Song's critique of Western reductionistic theology merits our attention today:

> When emotion takes leave of the heart as the seat of human spirit, our theology becomes an emotional theology. . . . On the other hand, when reason is separated from the heart, there emerges a cold theology that tries to penetrate the mystery of God with a cold logic.[37]

Song sees the heart as transrational and beyond the worldviews that "intuit the mystery of Being" where neither reason nor emotion alone can grasp. We perceive and encounter this Being, *agape*, at the crossroad of creation and redemption.[38] A theology of heart, therefore, offers ample missiological implications for overcoming what Paul G. Hiebert addressed as the two-tiered Neo-Platonic theology of religion and science that creates an excluded middle. In the West, the middle level offers guidance to the unknown future, the crises of present life, and the unknown past. This middle level began disappearing during the seventeenth and eighteenth centuries with the rise of Cartesian dualism in science and religion.[39] The consequence of the polemic worldview includes secularization on the one hand and the rise of the charismatic movement on the other.

In constructing a holistic and inclusive middle theology, I therefore argue for a theology of heart that also extends to the outer contexts of ecology and the planet. Sallie McFague's planetary theology helpfully bridges the missing link of theology and extends the concept of stewardship to time, resource, talents, and nature. In *Life Abundant*, McFague refers to humanity's alienation from nature and self. This alienation leads to "apartheid thinking,"

---

37. Song, *Third-Eye Theology*, 56–57.
38. Ibid., 72–73.
39. Paul G. Hiebert, *Anthropological Reflections on Missiological Issues* (Grand Rapids: Baker Books, 1994), 196–97.

"belief that our lives and our economy exist apart from nature."[40] It is impossible to see how individuals or the human community can prosper apart from a sustainable planet. In contrast to an atomistic value system, God's ecosystem is synergistic, and all of creation is interdependent. McFague warned a decade ago that neoliberal economic policy would ravage God's earth. Therefore, an alternative economic paradigm of the household economy, the *oikos*, maximizes the optimal functioning of the planet's gifts and services for all.[41] In the face of the global homogenization of human culture around maximum profit, our world begs for paradigmatic change, not merely a programmatic change.

This chapter first addressed the origin of the theological disconnect between humanity and nature, and, second, offered the yinist theology of heart as a holistic theological construct that contributes to overcoming the binary theology that results in anthropocentrism and the desacralization of nature. Ironically, history repeats itself. Taoism emerged during the time of Confucian domination and its corruption in ancient China. China today has become a global economic force and is consequently among the leading climate polluters, a condition that demands a retrieval of ancient Chinese cosmology. It is my belief that this cosmology of the Tao also applies to the realm of theology. For some time now, theological education has stood at the crossroad between the practical application of theology and its academic study. This tension has unfortunately led to an emphasis on the intellectual over the experiential, the yang over the yin. It is my hope that a holistic epistemology bringing a yinist balance may offer an integrative theological construct that honors all of God's creation for many generations to come.

---

40. Sallie McFague, *Life Abundant: Rethinking Theology and Economy for a Planet in Peril* (Minneapolis: Fortress Press, 2001), 118.
41. Ibid., 100.

• PART TWO •

Yinist Spirituality in the Bible

• 4 •

"If I Perish, I Perish"

Vashti and Esther

"See, I am sending you out like sheep into the midst of wolves; so be wise as serpents and innocent as doves."

Matthew 10:16

In the complex dynamics of human relationship systems, we inevitably find the embodiment of the identities of either the dissident Queen Vashti or the hyper-responsible Queen Esther, as described in the Old Testament book of Esther. The former is often labeled as the troublemaker and the latter as she who "can do no wrong." Growing up, I often played the role of Vashti. I was a child who dared to say "no" to my elders in a culture that excessively prizes the obedience of children. Conversely, all my female siblings inhabited the cultural script of "I obey, therefore I am." This was in stark contrast to my script of "I rebel, therefore I am." Conveniently, labeling my sisters as placating hypocrites, I charted out a one-dimensional path of integrity that centered on inner and outer congruence. No wonder I resonated with the Ugly Duckling story, feeling like an alien in my own home and culture. Hence, from very early on, I lived counterculturally by questioning accepted norms of greeting styles in the hierarchical structure of the Korean language. Basically, I had a crosscultural experience with the culture in which I was born.

Nonetheless, through my mother's fervent prayers, I finally experienced God's love during a college student retreat. From that time forward, there were numerous mentors in my life who played crucial roles in my spiritual formation and academic life. Yet despite my many teachers and allies, I was ill equipped to face the wolves of the world. I was vulnerable and in need of examples of women effectively confronting patriarchal subjugation. I found those role models in chapter 1 of the book of Esther, where Vashti and Esther stood out to me as complementary approaches to resisting oppression.

In the book of Esther, I discovered the interweaving narratives of these two extraordinary women—that of Queen Vashti and that of Queen Esther, who ultimately supplants her. Although the two women appear dissimilar, they share unlikely commonalities. Both are liberated from the internalization of the patriarchal oppression that perpetuates the vicious cycle of subjugating women. Both women resort to an "if I perish, I perish" (Esther 4:16) resolution in confronting the patriarchal abuse of power, but in their own unique ways: Vashti by bucking the system, and Esther by milking, if not teasing, the system. The banquets are the arena in which the dance of power—moving forward, against, and away—is played out by King Ahasuerus, Queen Vashti, and Queen Esther.

My focus here is on the banquet rituals that reveal the twists and turns of the power dynamics in Ahasuerus's court. Despite its ancient context, I find ample contemporary parallels. I hope that unpacking the rich narratives of the key players in the book of Esther will benefit many emerging Asian American church women leaders who have been indoctrinated by evangelical church culture to be innocent as doves, yet lack the wisdom of serpents (Matthew 10:16). The internalization of patriarchal church culture relegates many hard-working women leaders to second-class status while elevating male leadership as the ideal. Consequently, many women in the church find it difficult to accept the legitimacy of female leadership, perhaps most notably in the form of female pastors.

When does an Asian American evangelical woman begin realizing that some crucial skills are missing from her toolbox as a church leader? When she finds herself lacking a serpent-like shrewdness as she realizes that she has been thrown in the middle of a system of wolves. The only script she learned is to be "innocent" as a dove, but this inevitably makes her prey to the institution's wolf-like culture. Without any foreknowledge or forewarning about the system, she remains vulnerable to the schemes that are designed in the wolves' best interests. I was once one of those evangelical women, innocent and idealistically driven for the sake of living out God's sacred calling.

In looking back at my own experience and the trials and errors I encountered, I believe that it was my innocence that ultimately harmed me. Even after my eyes were opened to the political jungle, I had no mentor to help me maneuver the system effectively. Plunged into a pool to sink or swim, I resorted to bucking the system altogether. What I lacked were the divergent options of teasing, taming, and even milking the system. As sheep, directly confronting the wolves can be fatal and requires the embrace of an "if I perish, I perish" mindset. But without a reasonable probability of success, innocence without shrewdness only leaves one as easy prey for the wolves. Taming the wolves, on the other hand, requires the harmony of both innocence (yin) and shrewdness (yang), something that Jesus emphasized when he commissioned his disciples.

The outcome of bucking the system is ultimately the denial of access to the system itself. Thus, those who resort to this tactic are most often forced to exit, giving up even the limited positions they hold. This approach ushers one into a season of shedding everything to which one is attached. Nonetheless, from the shedding of the old wool, a new wool emerges. It was only from this course of vulnerable soul-searching that I finally understood the vital importance of working the system, even being willing to tame or tease it if necessary, for the sake of the common good.

The Drama of the Power Banquets

The banquets, hosted by King Ahasuerus, Queen Vashti, and Queen Esther, unravel both the accumulation and objectification of power in the patriarchal palace. Ahasuerus's annual banquet is held as an opulent display of all of his military and material acquisitions, which also include the queen as another possession. The book *Nurturing Peace*, edited by Deenabandhu Manchala, documents the power dynamics of such a display:

A significant feature of the exercise of power in societies is that it is often encountered in structures that exist and operate on the basis of the objectification of power (e.g. authority, law, forces), its internalization (e.g. loyalty, duty, fear of sanction) and the accumulation of the means required to wield it (e.g. money, resources, technology). Such structures of power appear to exist by accumulating and processing the means to legitimize and perpetuate themselves.[1]

Both Vashti and Esther subversively eschew the passive internalization of the accumulative power of the king as demonstrated by his banquet. Exasperated with patriarchal objectification, Vashti hosts her own banquet for the palace women while refusing to attend Ahasuerus's banquet as just another display item. Later, Esther, outwardly innocent and inwardly shrewd, begins her resistance by calling for a collective fast. She then meticulously executes a series of banquets and successfully thwarts Haman's genocidal plot against her people. Esther's subversive use of the banquet was not conceived in a vacuum but appears to have been inspired by Vashti and emboldened by the spirituality of collective fasting. Thus, in the book of Esther, the dramas of bucking, hijacking, teasing, and milking the system all unfold around the multiple banquet rituals. We will examine Ahasuerus's banquet first.

The King's Banquet: Accumulative Power

It is beyond my imagination to comprehend King Ahasuerus's banquet. A showcase of his material wealth and military might, the banquet lasted seven days and was followed "for many days, one hundred eighty days in all" by the display of the kingdom's wealth and power to all the officials from the surrounding region (Esther 1:4). All of the glory of Ahasuerus's kingdom is put on public display, all while wine and food flowed freely for over six months!

---

1. Deenabandhu Manchala, *Nurturing Peace: Theological Reflections on Overcoming Violence* (Geneva: World Council of Churches Publication, 2005), 41.

On the seventh day of his banquet, when Ahasuerus was in high spirits from wine, he commanded the seven eunuchs to bring before him Queen Vashti, "for she was fair to behold." She was ordered to present herself, "wearing the royal crown," before the many drunken men toward the end of their gluttonous party (1:11). But Vashti refused to be another object displayed to the crowd. Instead, she hosted her own party for the palace women, who were in fact also the king's possessions! The queen's absence from the king's banquet infuriated Ahasuerus, and he burned with anger (1:10–12).

Vashti's refusal is an extraordinary one, especially when the consequences of her move against Ahasuerus's command entails all kinds of persecution, if not death. Often, the anger of the powerful intimidates the subordinate, silencing them, which then perpetuates the system of injustice. The powerless, fearing any further victimization, are often forced to placate the anger of the oppressor. Conditioned by the drive toward survival, the subordinate ensures the ease of the powerful at all costs, even as they themselves give up the right to feel any offense as human beings. Vashti was a threat to the patriarchal culture of ancient Persia. Today, a woman like her, one who defies the vicious cycle of female subjugation, is a threat to patriarchal Christianity.

Vashti's Banquet

Along with her refusal to obey King Ahasuerus's command to attend his banquet, Queen Vashti also hosts a banquet for the palace women in the house of the king (1:9). According to Chloe Sun, a Hebrew Bible scholar at Logos Evangelical Seminary, the Hebrew construction of Esther 1:9 indicates two important characteristics about Vashti's banquet. "Also" is placed in an emphatic position before the name Vashti, suggesting that the content of the verse is unusual.[2] Another emphatic structure is in the reversal of verb and subject. Sun stresses that in Hebrew, the verb is usually placed before the subject. Yet in 1:9, the verb is placed after the subject to

---

2. "Also" is the word used in the NIV; the NRSV uses "Furthermore."

further indicate the unusual circumstances of a queen holding a banquet for the women.

The direct English translation of 1:9 reads, "Also Vashti, the queen, made a feast for the women in the royal house which belonged to King Ahasuerus (Xerxes in Persian)." From the double emphatic construction in the Hebrew text, Sun deduces that 1:9 indicates "a contrast between Vashti's banquet and the king's, and also that Vashti is up to something."[3]

Obviously, Vashti's refusal to obey Ahasuerus's drunken command, made while "merry with wine," and then hosting her own banquet for the palace women require amazing courage and signify an alternative response to patriarchal subjugation by willingly choosing death over life. This could be construed as "bucking the system" with the full understanding that it could cost Vashti her life all the while winning her dignity as a human being, even if that dignity may last only a few moments.

I also faced circumstances that forced me to weigh the costs of choosing dignity over self-preservation. As witness to a racist action in a nearly all-white boardroom, I knew that speaking out could cost me my job. The events unfolded as the only male person of color in the room was presenting a multicultural vision of the institution. I watched as he was belittled by unfairly harsh questions from the all-white floor, who questioned the validity of his presentation. One detractor declared, "Who are you to tell us whether we are multicultural or not?" It was a comment blind to its own illogicality. The detractor held firm to his fundamental framework of power and authority. The establishment, as employers, could not allow their subjects, the employed, to define the parameters of their own identity.

This was my first real-life encounter with such blatant institutional racism. As the only woman of color in the room, I found myself deeply offended, and I was compelled to name what I saw. As I articulated my experience, the power holder of the room labeled

---

3. "Ahasuerus" is the Hebrew form of an Old Persian name. "Xerxes" is the Greek form of the same name (consultation with Hebrew Bible scholar Chloe Sun for Hebrew nuances in Esther 1:9, August 7, 2007).

me as the offensive one, much like the little boy in "The Emperor's New Clothes." The response I received from my peers regarding my action was, "You pounded a nail into your own coffin." Balancing the cost of calling out the CEO's abuse of power with the consequences of overlooking the injustice I witnessed, I chose integrity over holding on to a job that had, by that time, lost its meaning.

It was Vashti's example that emboldened me. Although I lacked Vashti's savvy in community organizing, people from the margins offered their support in my struggle. How could I live with myself if I chose to overlook injustice as it occurred before my eyes? Even if I was not the direct object of the ridicule, as a woman of color, I could not pretend to be deaf and blind to what was said and done. In a dehumanizing moment, one is confronted with the decision to subjugate by denial or to resort to an "if I perish, I perish" state.

There are moments in life when one has to call it as it is to maintain the integrity of one's soul, even if that means great personal loss. In such a case, silence is not a sign of virtue but a sign of cowardice. As Mordecai forewarned Queen Esther: "For if you keep silence at such a time as this, relief and deliverance will rise for the Jews from another quarter . . ." (4:14). But breaking the silence does not always guarantee immediate deliverance, relief, or justice. Sometimes one dies without seeing the results and finds that one's role was to plant the seeds for future deliverance. Perhaps it is for this reason that many breadwinners choose to overlook injustice rather than to risk their livelihoods in order to call out injustice. Thus, both men and women in the workplace often advise others to "choose your battles."

The Fearful Responses of the Powerful

From King Ahasuerus down to his officials, the patriarchal perception of threat from Queen Vashti's refusal of the king's command, as well as the hosting of her own women's party, results in a series of defensive strategies. When one reads the first chapter of the book of Esther, the contemporary parallels are astounding. There is a deep contrast between the fear of the power holder and the courage of the powerless. The objectification of power refers to authority, law, and force that legitimatize the maintenance of power that benefits the powerful. Consequently, the powerless remain disenfranchised by law and thus have no access to justice. Those who never question the law are the privileged who have been well served by the law, whereas the powerless cannot but be suspicious of the law since they have been subject to its injustice.

In his anger, Ahasuerus first seeks council from "the sages who knew the laws" (1:13). "'According to the law, what is to be done to Queen Vashti?'" asks the king (1:15). From Ahasuerus's and the patriarchs' reactions, one can see the impact of Vashti's defiance. Particularly notice Ahasuerus's counselors' fear that Vashti's resistance will become contagious:

> Then Memucan said in the presence of the king and the officials, "Not only has Queen Vashti done wrong to the king, but also to all the officials and all the peoples who are in all the provinces of King Ahasuerus. For this deed of the queen will be made known to all women, causing them to look with contempt on their husbands, since they will say, 'King Ahasuerus commanded Queen Vashti to be brought before him, and she did not come.'" (1:16–17)

Deposing Vashti from her position as queen is not enough. In fear of the ripple effect of Vashti's action, Ahasuerus, his nobles, and the council put their heads together, utilizing all their available assets, from legal and astrological resources (1:13). They legislate a royal decree, essentially a women's code of conduct, that reads, "all women will give honor to their husbands, high and low alike" (1:20), adding that "every man should be master in his own house" (1:22). The thorough measures taken to prevent the ripple effect of Vashti's behavior on all the women of the land testify to the power of one woman's courage and conviction, sending shock waves through the establishment.

On behalf of all women, Vashti dares to refuse to remain a "sheep"—a prop for patriarchal pleasure. She demonstrates the power of women united—a liberating power that stands in contrast to the powerlessness of women divided, and thus conquered.

In a sense, Vashti can be seen as the first to host an organized prophetic women's banquet. There are plenty of reasons why the patriarchs are threatened and did not want to open the floodgates of a potential threat to their male-dominant system. The power of the subjugated is evident in Vashti's willingness to die for her cause. No external power can penetrate into such inner power of letting go—the "if I perish, I perish" conviction that turns the tables of power around.

In my identification with Vashti, I also learned that much of leadership requires the art of milking, if not teasing, the system for the common good. Bucking the system has to be a last resort when all other available resources are exhausted, as Vashti's case testifies. It was not until I lost the job I loved that I truly understood the need for diverse leadership in efforts to promote the marginalized. It requires cultivating finesse, skill, and most of all, a character of courage accompanied by perseverance. It invites one on a meandering journey in the interstitial space. This is a space mastered by Esther, who exemplifies a similar but different approach to Vashti's in the system of power.

Esther's Banquet Series

With Queen Vashti deposed, King Ahasuerus stages what is essentially a beauty pageant to replace her. The Jewish woman, Esther, known in Hebrew as Hadassah, wins Ahasuerus's contest and enters the enemy's palace as its queen. She thus rises from the ranks of an oppressed minority into the highest position for a woman in that country. Ahasuerus demonstrates the extent of his favor for Esther through an elaborate installation banquet:

> Then the king gave a great banquet to all his officials and ministers—"Esther's banquet." He also granted a holiday to the provinces, and gave gifts with royal liberality. (2:18)

Once again, Ahasuerus displays his wealth and power by hosting a banquet that includes generous gifts to the attendees. For Ahasuerus, the banquet signifies the reshaping of the tarnished image of the queenship, but for Esther, queenship eventually opens the door for her to access the king's wealth, power, and other resources. Esther will eventually use Ahasuerus's own power machinery to execute her mission to save her people from genocide at the hands of Ahasuerus and especially of his vizier, Haman.

Esther's cousin, Mordecai, sends a message to her to appear before Ahasuerus to try to prevent the genocide from happening, but Esther finds it impossible to appear before the king without his summons. All the people of the royal provinces know that anyone who approaches the king in the inner court without being summoned was to be summarily put to death. The only way to stay this execution was by decree of Ahasuerus himself, manifest through the extension of his gold scepter. Thirty days having passed since Esther was called to go to Ahasuerus, she struggles to find a solution to her dilemma (4:11).

Upon Mordecai's second urging, Esther turns to God. She begins a three-day ritual fast, saying, "I and my maids will also fast as you do. After that I will go to the king, though it is against the law; and if I perish, I perish" (4:16). At this particular moment, Esther no longer relies on Mordecai but takes the matter to a higher level, seeking God's guidance and wisdom to carry out her mission. Tracing its origins back to shamanism and Buddhism, fasting has long been a favored spiritual discipline among Korean Christians. It is often an expression of a desperate plea to God in times of crisis and life transitions.

Empowered by this communal fasting, Esther is transformed into a woman of resolution. Once she embraces her calling, even the risk of death cannot curtail her God-given mission. On the third day of her fasting, she courageously appears before Ahasuerus without his summons. Esther stands in the inner court of the palace wearing her royal robes (5:1). It is a real moment of "if I perish, I perish." Placing her fate in God's hands, Esther awaits Ahasuerus's response. Instead of carrying out the expected execution, Ahasuerus makes an exception. He asks, "What is it, Queen Esther? What is your request? It shall be given you, even to the half of my kingdom" (5:3).

It can be surmised that Esther, having lived in the palace for an extended period of time, is well aware of Vashti's infamous banquet. It is then no surprise that Esther, like Vashti, also hosts her own subversive series of banquets that turn the status quo upside down. Both women risked death for organizing banquets—Vashti, by her refusal to appear at Ahasuerus's banquet and hosting her own, and Esther by appearing before Ahasuerus without his summons. Thus, both acted with the rare courage of "if I perish, I perish." They risked their lives for a specific mission: Vashti, for declaring the dignity of the palace women and thus for all women at that time, and Esther for rescuing her people from impending genocide.

Esther manages to use the tool of Ahasuerus's display of power—the banquet—to reverse the fate of her people. Esther's plan is well on its way when Ahasuerus begs to know her petition. With the wine flowing, Esther ensures the king's favor and invites him for another banquet. She replies:

> This is my petition and request: If I have won the king's favor, and if it pleases the king to grant my petition and fulfill my request, let the king and Haman come tomorrow to the banquet that I will prepare for them, and then I will do as the king has said. (5:7–8)

Esther's poise in crisis kept her enemy, Haman, clueless. In fact, he went home "happy and in good spirits" (5:9), boasting to his friends and wife that he was the only person Queen Esther had invited to come with the king to her banquet (5:12).

Reversal of Fortune

Meanwhile, King Ahasuerus is restless and sleepless after Queen Esther's first banquet. He must have been wondering what her petition might be. At that moment, he orders the nighttime reading of "the book of records, the annals" (6:1). He finds that it was Mordecai who rescued his life from an assassination plot. Ahasuerus asks who is in the court at that time, and learns that "Haman had just entered the outer court of the king's palace to speak to the king about having Mordecai hanged on the gallows that he had prepared for him" (6:4). When Ahasuerus asks, "What shall be done for the man whom the king wishes to honor?" Haman, full of delusions that the king must be referring to him, describes how he himself would like to be honored (6:7–9). Ahasuerus then commands Haman:

> Quickly, take the robes and the horse, as you have said, and do so to the Jew Mordecai who sits at the king's gate. Leave out nothing that you have mentioned. (6:10)

Already the perfect prelude to the second banquet of Esther has unfolded. The reversal of injustice and hatred, which will reach its climax at Esther's second banquet, has begun. The drama continues even after Esther pleads with Ahasuerus to stop Haman from killing her people. In his desperation, Haman digs his grave even deeper by throwing himself "on the couch where Esther was reclining" (7:8). Ahasuerus returns from the garden after cooling from his anger at Haman only to find him in an even more egregious state of disrespect. Ahasuerus exclaims, "Will he even assault the queen in my presence, in my own house?" (7:8).

Through the twists and turns of Esther's story, the contrast between the characters of Haman and Esther peaks. Cautiously, Esther double checks her risk and solicits assurance of Ahasuerus's favor. The combination of humility, poise, and courage in the midst of impending genocide exemplifies the depth of her spirituality. After all, leadership involves precise execution with poise of a mission at the right moment in times of crisis. As Esther's savvy increases, the boastful Haman turns into a pitiful coward. No longer do we see a timid Hadassah (2:7) but instead a true queen of great stature.

Neither the removal of the enemy nor the granting of his estate is enough for Esther. She is not sidetracked by the temptation of power but focuses on her mission—the survival of her people. She executes a reversal of injustice by changing the law. As Ray Bakke remarks, "Esther teaches us that it's not enough just to repent for sin. It's systemic, and the law has to change."[4] Although Vashti became the victim of the legal decree, Esther meticulously utilizes

---

4. Richard A. Kauffman, "Apostle to the City, Part 2" (interview with urban expert Ray Bakke), *Christianity Today*, March 3, 1997, https://www.christianitytoday.com.

the law to assure the safety of her people. In seeking legal protection for her people, Esther demonstrates boldness dressed in feminine vulnerability, falling at the feet of Ahasuerus, "weeping and pleading with him" (8:3). She begs him:

> If it pleases the king, and if I have won his favor, and if the thing seems right before the king, and I have his approval, let an order be written to revoke the letters devised by Haman son of Hammedatha the Agagite, which he wrote giving orders to destroy the Jews who are in all the provinces of the king. For how can I bear to see the calamity that is coming on my people? Or how can I bear to see the destruction of my kindred? (8:5–6).

Fueled by a patriotic mission to rescue her people from annihilation, Esther wisely mixes boldness with tenderness. In response to her pleading, Ahasuerus commands the legislation of another decree in his name, and Mordecai himself ends up writing and sealing it (8:10).

With her cousin Mordecai's mentorship, Esther, originally innocent as a dove, becomes shrewd like a serpent in executing her mission. This transition from dove to serpent occurs once she realizes her role in the grander scheme of things. This sense of destiny makes it possible for her to tame the system of the "wolves"—the king and his officials in this case.

Commemoration of the Days of Purim

Queen Esther organizes the Hebrews to fast and pray before executing her tasks, which can only be viewed as subversive by the powers that be in that time and place: "In the twelfth month, which is the month of Adar, on the thirteenth day, when the king's command and edict were about to be executed, on the very day when the enemies of the Jews hoped to gain power over them, but which had been changed to a day when the Jews would gain power over their foes" (9:1). To this day, the Jews remember Esther's successful efforts to save her people by observing Purim: the day of feasting and the day of joy. What a long-lasting legacy Esther established for the Jewish people! She risked wisely and executed boldly, working the system by teasing it and milking it, for the sake of her people. Moreover, none of her actions were in service of her own ego. She wore her queenship not in pride but as the necessary tool for justice. Too often have I seen titles and positions become hollow uniforms, as if they were the true identity of their bearers. Esther, however, managed a most rare and effective combination, maintaining the humility of her origins while embracing the strength and power of her new position.

Subversive Banquets

The banquet system served as a tool for the propagation of the existing power system. Queen Esther's subversive use of this system exemplifies her cunning redirection of power in favor of the formerly oppressed. Successfully accomplishing such a task requires maturity, depth of spirituality, conviction, patience, and courage. The book of Esther contains many types of banquets—King Ahasuerus's annual banquet for the patriarchs and foreign nobles, Queen Vashti's palace women's resistance banquet, and Esther's series of subversive banquets. At all of these events, the drama of social stratification is unveiled and depicts movement "toward," "against," and "away from" the power structure as represented in the arrangement of the guest list, the seating arrangement, and so forth.

Ahasuerus's banquet serves as a mere beauty pageant for parading his possessions. Vashti's banquet works "against" and "away" from Ahasuerus and leads to the immediate removal of her access to him. This leaves her vulnerable to the patriarchal system and its whims. Vashti's palace women's banquet is perceived by the patriarchs as a threat to their misogynistic power over all the women in the kingdom and leads to her dethroning and removal as queen. In a manner of speaking, Vashti's movement toward standing up for herself and the subjugated palace women displays the unusual courage and strength of the "if I perish, I perish" statement. Experiencing life as a human being rather than a royal object is worthy, even if it lasts only momentarily. Thus, the palace women under

Vashti's leadership buck the patriarchal system and choose to put their lives on the line by their actions.

In reviewing Vashti and Esther's approach to the system, I have learned that yielding a "soft outside" (yin) while maintaining integrity of soul, represented as a "solid inside" (yang), takes enormous strength. I seek the integration of the two in such a way that the system to which I belong benefits those most vulnerable. I used to believe that people who exhibited a soft exterior were weak. I was not able to perceive the strength, the "solidity," inside that person. It has been a long journey to value the wholeness of the yin/yang interplay. I also learned that in contrast to direct confrontation, the seemingly subversive and indirect style demonstrated by Esther works well when dealing with powerful, but insecure, systems. On the other hand, without a pioneer like Vashti to start the upheaval, unjust systems run by wolves will remain unchallenged, thus recycling the burden of the subjugated to amuse the powerful and pander to their sense of entitlement.

I can see why Esther is one of the most preferred biblical names for Asian Americans. "Face-saving" is one of the most important concepts adhered to by this group. There is always some degree of face-saving maneuvering in social interactions among the pan-Asian American groups, and one can easily detect subtle efforts geared toward protecting the other's dignity and one's own pride. Culturally embedded face-saving mechanisms can have both positive and negative effects. The positive effect involves the protection of the relationship. Meanwhile, the negative effects are the burying of conflict or an indirect address, potentially leading to emotional implosion, if not explosion. Open and direct communication of disagreement is perceived as offensive. Passive aggressiveness flourishes in Asian American culture, although face-saving mechanisms are not a uniquely Asian cultural phenomenon. They also exist in Western European and Caucasian cultures, but usually in lesser degrees.

The book of Esther contains dramatic twists and turns centering on a variety of royal banquets, beginning with King Ahasuerus's, followed by Queen Vashti's, and concluding with Queen Esther's.

Esther takes on Vashti's role as resistor when she embraces her mission to rescue her people. Both Vashti and Esther demonstrate remarkable courage: the former by bucking the system, the latter by milking the system. The cultural and countercultural roles skillfully balanced by these two women provide rich narratives for contemporary Asian American women leaders. We Asian American women also face dominant patriarchal systems both within the church and in society at large. These systems work to define and confine women's roles. The creation of an empowering system across gender, class, ethnicity, and race is crucial to the health of the body of Christ.

One danger of an all-or-nothing ideology is the demonization of the other as "all bad" while characterizing ourselves as "all good." Asian American churchwomen need to honor Vashtis who, by sacrificing their positions, have paved the way for many other women to fulfill their dreams and life missions for the common good. Without Vashti, there can be no Esther.

"Good women," as defined by the patriarchs, are those who remain harmless to the patriarchal establishment. Many women internalize this definition, criticizing confrontational Vashtis while upholding harmless Esthers. As with Bathsheba, the historian records that Vashti recovers her influence through her son, who inherits the throne once Esther falls out of Ahasuerus's favor. The only way for women to exercise power under the patriarchal system was to use their sons. Vashti, like Bathsheba, wields her power over her son in order to beat the patriarchal system that silences women's voices.

Interestingly, under the oppression of Haman, Mordecai is able to exercise his influence through Esther's queenship to thwart the impending genocide of the Hebrews. I commend both of these exemplary ancient women whose courage inspires people under siege: Vashti, humanizing her fellow palace women; and Esther, delivering the Hebrew people from genocide. Once she understands the royal palace system and the power of her position, Esther is not content to merely win an elaborate beauty pageant. Under the mentorship of Mordecai, Esther becomes a woman with a mission.

When Asian American women first embark on leadership roles, what most plagues us is our lack of a support network and political savvy. In other words, we don't have an understanding of how to "work the system." Innocent as Esther was before her cousin Mordecai awakened her to a sacred mission, Asian American women leaders are unnecessarily placed in harm's way. It requires mentors like Mordecai to see oneself in context, to fully understand the position in which one is placed and to discern the proper timing.

There is no apprenticeship in learning to negotiate the inevitable challenges that come with being a woman in leadership. My recommendation to Asian American evangelical churchwomen is to identify mentors who, like Mordecai, can help to navigate the patriarchal terrain of the institution one serves. Without such guidance, Asian American women leaders will undermine their effectiveness in ministry. For this reason, Asian American Women on Leadership (AAWOL) has decided to share our leadership journey with the upcoming generation of Asian American women leaders so they may be able to foster sustainable leadership in the midst of the wolves in and out of the system. AAWOL hopes to pass on both Vashti's and Esther's examples. The hard-earned lessons from both women serve as vital and necessary models for today's Asian American Christian leaders. These lessons resonate deeply from my own experience where I learned from Vashti how to take a painful hit silently after resisting injustices and from Esther how to risk tenderly and wisely.

The Dance of Encounter (John 4)

In this chapter, I will analyze the mentorship provided by Jesus in his liberation of the Samaritan woman at the well, as described in John 4. But I will first describe my own encounter with a mentor whose guidance was invaluable to me during my formation as a theologian.

When it comes to surrounding myself with spiritual giants, I am greedy. There exists nothing more significant in my life than my encounters with key leaders who have enriched my journey. At the right divine moments, God provided these figures through both friendships and Christian communities. As Jesus's dialogical encounter with the Samaritan woman liberated her from her bondage, I have also been liberated from my own shortcomings through the mentors I've had. One of them is my mentor from my doctoral program, the late Dr. Paul Hiebert, who recognized my gifts and affirmed them when I was still clueless. While it was my parents who initially provided me with wings, it was Paul Hiebert who encouraged me to fly toward my professional dreams.

Behind every leader are numerous mentors who have equipped them in ways they alone could not have done. From experiences with my own mentors, I have observed that a mentor foresees a mentee's potential and guides him/her to reach his/her God-given calling in life. I have had several important women mentors who have guided me along my path, women who have been invaluable in teaching me how to navigate a profession dominated by men. But in this chapter, I am compelled and honored to address my male mentor, Dr. Paul Hiebert.

As a third-generation Mennonite missionary to India, Paul finished high school in India and came to the United States for college and graduate school. Once he finished his degrees, he returned to India as an anthropologist and missionary. His missionary work was curtailed because of his wife Fran's illness. They returned to the United States where Paul taught at Fuller Theological Seminary. It was at Fuller that I spotted his Worldview and Worldview Change class syllabus displayed in the bookstore. This led me to enroll in his class and eventually to pursue doctoral work under him. My own teaching style was shaped by Paul's doctoral seminar. It was during these Friday morning seminars that I saw how his methods closely resembled Jesus's dialogical teaching method.

Paul's seminars would typically begin with a student's presentation of a paper, which prompted rich dialogue. Then at the end, he would draw his famous diagrams, elevating our work beyond our imagination. Facilitating dialogue among twelve doctoral students, Paul's teaching was indeed a life-transforming experience. He modeled radical discipleship in both word and deed. I still remember him inviting doctoral students to his home to cook for us, offering meaningful and personal table fellowship. He must now be rejoicing in heaven with his wife, a reunion he eagerly awaited. Both Paul and Fran had advocated for women's leadership in the church, opening doors for many women both at Fuller Theological Seminary and Trinity Evangelical School. With his sharp mind and cross-cultural empathy and humility as a third-culture person himself, Paul transformed my life through the many rich dialogues we shared. Likewise, there is another woman who finds her God-given calling through a dialogical encounter, the Samaritan woman with Jesus at the well. In this chapter, we will continue our analysis of John 4 (which we began in chapter 2, pp. 30–21) with a focus on the "third space" provided by such an encounter.

Encounter at the Well

Thirsty after a long walk in the desert, Jesus approaches the Samaritan woman at the well and asks for a drink. The woman's response to Jesus's surprising treatment reveals his unconventional nature. Shocked by his request, she replies, "How is it that you, a Jew, ask a drink of me, a woman of Samaria?" (4:9). Jesus's behavior warrants her shock. The cultural norms of her time prohibited their interaction along both religious and gender lines. These behavioral rules were "sacred cows," making it inconceivable that a Jewish man could approach a lone, Samaritan woman for a drink, deeming her worthy to meet his needs. His request unravels all the Samaritan woman's "isms"—racism, sexism, classism, religionism, and regionalism. Jesus's actions shake her from the doldrums of her ordinary life and create an opening for an in-depth engagement.

But her response to his request discloses both surprise and anxiety. In addition to her shock at his disregard for cultural norms, the woman must have been astonished by the way she was treated as a subject rather than an object. Stepping out of her secure boundaries, no matter how oppressive they may be, demands an adjustment and thus induces anxiety. In this discourse, she actively uncovers deep-seated issues; and the more the woman engages in dialogue, the closer her encounter with Jesus becomes. Jesus brilliantly thaws the woman's frozen self-perception that has been shaped by conventional prescriptions. A deep healing surfaces as she discovers herself as a subject rather than an object. Within their exchange, a bridge is forged between the partitioned sides of Jews and Samaritans, males and females, previous and present prophets. Jesus understands the woman's readiness to deal with the well within herself.

Radicalization: From Object to Subject

A basic assumption on which Paulo Freire operates is that a person's ontological vocation should be as a subject taking action, thus transforming the subject's own world. In this process, the subject "moves towards ever new possibilities of fuller and richer life individually and collectively."[1]

Likewise, the Samaritan woman becomes liberated from being an

---

1. Paulo Freire, *Pedagogy of the Oppressed*, trans. Myra Bergman Ramos (New York: Seabury, 1970), 13.

object of oppression to a "subject" through a dialogical encounter with Jesus, who says that "those who drink of the water that I will give them will never be thirsty. The water that I will give will become in them a spring of water gushing up to eternal life" (John 4:14). Jesus pours out for her the gift of living water, and her spirit is regenerated. She becomes the integrated person she was created to be.

Freire is right in asserting that no matter how a person may have been silenced, he or she may be renewed through dialogical encounter.

Moving from Exterior to Interior

Once Jesus progressed in the dialogue to the point in which the woman began to see herself as a subject, he moves the woman to a journey inward. At this time, a surprising reversal takes place. It is the Samaritan woman, not Jesus, who then asks for water. "Sir, give me this water so that I won't get thirsty and have to keep coming here to draw water," she asks (4:15). Confronting Jesus with questions, the Samaritan woman's request is met with deeper challenges. Jesus reveals her vulnerabilities by asking the woman to "Go, call your husband and come back" (4:16).

A most important aspect of the woman's liberation process comes from how Jesus deals with the woman's response, "I have no husband" (4:17). Jesus affirms her reply: "You are right when you say you have no husband. The fact is you have had five husbands, and the man you now have is not your husband. What you have just said is quite true" (4:18).

Why does Jesus affirm her twice here? Perhaps Jesus was revealing to her that since her present partner is not her husband, she needs to move forward. Responding to Jesus's double affirmation, the woman in turn affirms Jesus as prophetic, admitting to the truthfulness of Jesus's words (4:19).

At this point, one is struck by the beauty of the dance of dialogue in the story. What could have been met with resistance manifests the authenticity of speaking the truth and thus transformation. Jesus models his own vulnerability, and now the woman is able to deal with her most vulnerable self. In response to Jesus's acceptance and affirmation, she also affirms Jesus. In her most vulnerable moment of self-disclosure, her eyes are open and she begins to see the true nature of Jesus (4:26–29). Her eyes have seen the Messiah.

What begins as an exterior theological discourse from a distance is transformed into an interior theological encounter. At this moment, the woman discovers her true self; she is able to tap into her interior well. The external, utilitarian well becomes a fountain within. The journey of an amazing transformation begins. She no longer shies away from people but turns the whole village upside down as she herself is turned inside and out. Theology no longer functions at the cerebral level, but is now embodied.

The entire dialogical encounter portrays a most beautiful dance of reciprocity initiated by Jesus and followed by the woman—poetry in motion reaching the peak of human potential. The questions and replies in the story illustrate the beauty and power of human dialogue, dynamically interwoven—the pinnacle of hope in the midst of despair.

Their dialogue leads to the restoration within her of the image of God. Revitalized, she leaves her jar at the well and runs out to her village, giving testimony as Jesus's first female evangelist. The power of such dialogical encounters is also depicted by Freire. He writes:

> Dialogue cannot exist, however, in the absence of a profound love for the world and for human [men]. The naming of the world, which is an act of creating and re-creation, is not possible if it is not infused with love. Love is at the same time the foundation of dialogue and dialogue itself.[2]

When loving dialogue transcends all conventional prejudice and stereotypes, a recovery and re-creation of God's image is possible, no matter how broken a person may be. It is the loving and patient process of dialogue and spending time together despite fatigue that fosters the transformation of hearts. Aren't we all in need of such an encounter as this in our fast-paced modern life? Leadership

---

2. Ibid., 77–78.

today is especially in need of such encounters, with our overfocus on management at the expense of human engagement.

Although some may argue about the gulf of time, space, and culture between the text and today's context, I hold that the fundamental principles of Jesus are a metanarrative that applies to all humanity across all time. No one can deny the fact we live in a broken world full of wounded people pleading for restoration. Therefore, this chapter seeks to explore how Jesus liberates a woman in bondage through a dialogical encounter and what that encounter means for us today.

The Power of Denial

While the transformed woman is engaged in her new mission, the disciples are literally out to lunch. Even when they return they choose disengagement. Shocked by their teacher's forbidden interaction with the Samaritan woman, the disciples resort to denial. They deny themselves the transforming moment that leads to true action. Meanwhile, the formerly imprisoned woman is freed from social, racial, and theological taboos. Her theology no longer serves as a boundary but as a liberating tool.

Like the woman at the well, I have been blessed in my encounters with theological mentors who saw my potential when I could not. That is why I am able to testify to the power of education when it embodies the whole person. Theological educators need to stop by the well and rediscover the refreshing and life-generating fountain in the midst of academic life in the fast lane.

In our classes and churches there are many women and men who need fresh and living water in their spiritual wells, just as Jesus ignites the spirit of a prophet within the Samaritan woman. Immediately she is activated and begins to evangelize in her village. Like the disciples in the narrative, theological education in general lacks an understanding of its inherent power of transformation. It is focused on the head trips of theological debates, which rarely move people's hearts and surely not their feet.

Having served in both church and seminary settings, I discovered the power of transformational learning that touches the heart of the people. Yet false beliefs within institutions continually breed fragmentation and deprivation. This transformation only occurs when these false beliefs are broken down, allowing dialogical encounters to act as agents of change.

A Rationale for Developing a Third Space for Encounter

A nuts-and-bolts model of networking and partnership is needed to recast theological education in a new framework. This framework should take both experiential and theoretical approaches and treat them as two sides of one coin. My emphasis on the former stems from my experience of running a nonprofit organization, ISAAC (Innovative Space for Asian American Christianity), and the latter from my theological journey since 1981, which has run parallel with the ongoing postcolonial dialogue.

Positioning in a third space, one that is not dualistic but rather contains both "sides of the coin," is often accompanied by unpredictability, uncertainty, and confusion. However, it is this very unpredictability that allows the people of God to go into the wilderness, relying on manna and faith, with no reserves. In the intellectual and highly strategic world of academic culture, unpredictability and uncertainty are deemed undesirable. Nevertheless, they can be both challenging and rewarding, depending upon one's perspective.

As a nonprofit organization, ISAAC is positioned in a third space as free-standing, interdependent, intersectional, and interdisciplinary. It is both the academy and the church; it is both yin and yang. Forging partnerships from this third space presents challenges as well as opportunities. In transforming a network into potential partnerships, ISAAC confronts a myriad of power variables.

The first challenge involves issues of fame. Although no groups are impervious to the effects of celebrity, it has been my experience that Asian Americans gravitate especially to individuals and institutions that have name recognition, popular appeal, and establishment credibility. When an entity such as ISAAC does not embody these features, it becomes challenging to attract the attention of Asian Americans outside of ISAAC's immediate community. Yet, when ISAAC works under a mainstream institutional umbrella, it is susceptible to being directed by institutional agendas and interests.

The second challenge is a perceived power imbalance between specialty and hybridity. In the academy, specialty typically equals prestige. As postcolonial scholars (e.g., Homi K. Bhabha, Peter van Dommelen, etc.) elucidate, hybridity is not a simple fusion of new and old elements of ideology or practice but rather an ongoing development in relation to micro- and macrocontexts.

The third challenge is one of capital, both social and financial. As Sallie McFague[3] and Kwok Pui-lan[4] describe, the neoliberal economic takeover has virtually reduced human interactions and institutional survival to capital. The call for an alternative theological education to neoliberal education seems crucial.

The privilege of embarking on the task of theological education from a third space involves freedom to partner with diverse institutions creatively, both inside and outside of theological "palaces." There are many theologians inside such palaces who are resistant to the royal privilege of knowledge production provided by their location. Yet many are also unable or unwilling to champion significant change. Needless to say, for the insiders of the palace, change carries with it high stakes: politically, financially, and socially. Meanwhile, for the outsiders in the wilderness of the third space, the stakes are much more fluid.

The story of the woman at the well elucidates the third-space encounter. Here we see the initial back and forth of trial and error give way to a dance of reciprocity between Jesus and the Samaritan woman. In contrast to neoliberal theological institutions and curricula, Jesus's pedagogy invites us to an organic dialogue without overhead costs. An epistemological lens for approaching the texts is the yinist perspective, an interdependent yin/yang gestalt that covers both gender and nature.

Positioning one's mission in a third space requires sacrifice and faith because there is no blueprint except reliance on God's evolving intervention and daily manna. In the binary culture of the acad-

---

3. See Sallie McFague, *Life Abundant: Rethinking Theology and Economy for a Planet in Peril* (Minneapolis: Fortress Press, 2000), 75–97.
4. See Kwok Pui-lan, *Postcolonial Imagination and Feminist Theology* (Louisville, KY: Westminster John Knox Press, 2005), 7.

emy where strategic details of blueprint, planning, and outcome take high priority, working from the wilderness of a third space takes persistence. To become a bridging leader requires wisdom and learning through life's trials and errors. It takes, indeed, experiential learning beyond cognitive knowledge.

The Characteristics of a Third Space

As discussed earlier, the development of a third space that is conducive to the encounter is not simply exchanging the current status quo for its binary opposite. It requires an unusually deft openness to the totality of both divine and human experience. This effort begins with the establishing of a liminal space, an in-between state where the threshold of yin and yang are allowed to interact freely, where the interplay of structure and organisticity are given room to creatively generate novel experiences and relationships. I consider this the merging of divine encounters with institutional structure.

Within this third space, there is the inevitability of clashing worldviews. One such clash is between community and individualism, which can be characterized as between philanthropy and the culture of "winner takes all."

This example is a classic variation of the yin versus yang framework. One is receptive and vulnerable while the other is aggressive and confrontational. As Jesus models in his encounter with the Samaritan woman, this need not be an either/or proposition. Both the community and the individual can exist simultaneously. Jesus's approach dealt with the reality and necessity of both yin and yang energies. Jesus confronts the woman's truth while honestly engaging her in her experience. Jesus himself proceeds with openness and vulnerability, leading with his inferiority and weakness at the well. It was, after all, he who initially requested her help.

The benefits of working from a third space are rich and varied. At the most basic level, encounters in the wilderness embody a freedom, creativity, and adaptability that are difficult to engender in structured environments. As new challenges arise, the third space is able to respond quickly to those needs. This is especially valuable in time-limited and urgent matters. On the other side of the coin, when new opportunities are presented, working from the third space allows us to seize on these prospects without being bogged down by institutional channels. The result can be unprecedented grassroots coalition building and social movement. In ISAAC's case, we have been blessed with the capacity to develop bridges with the financial sector in our fifth symposium and between the Asian American and the African American church in our sixth symposium. For some time now, theological education has stood at the crossroads between the practical application of theology and its academic study. This tension has, unfortunately, led generally to an overemphasis on the intellectual over the experiential. It is my hope that Jesus's encounter with the woman at the well can serve as a profound model for the synthesis of these two positions, leaving neither behind but instead allowing both to be integrated harmoniously into a holistic framework that impacts both the academy and the church in deep and meaningful ways.

My Encounter with Paul Hiebert

I am grateful that God allowed me to encounter Paul Hiebert and his wife, Fran. They embodied radical discipleship that countered the pressures of conformity and a performance-driven culture. Their legacies of holistic teaching and mentoring continue through many of their students all over the world. After his wife passed away from breast cancer, Paul used his home for the communal housing of international doctoral students and even yielded his own bedroom to this cause. My last phone conversation with Paul interrupted a lunch at his house with some of these international students. Gladly, he let me interrupt, picking up our discussion from where we last left off. We had a nice forty-five-minute conversation, even while he had an oxygen device assisting his breathing. Paul embodied what it means to be a radical disciple. Through his example, I learned to be content living a countercultural life.

The Challenge of Leadership

Unlike the examples provided by Jesus and Paul Hiebert, educational values and their praxis often mirror monologue rather than dialogue. Even when introducing the importance of dialogue, it is done as a monologue, merely maintaining the status quo. In a one-sided educational setting, a communal encounter between teacher and learner and between learner and learner is often not feasible. Learning to monologue in educational institutions shapes many leaders in ministry to be talkers rather than deep listeners like Jesus, who tapped into the depth of the Samaritan woman's soul. No wonder we face leadership crises in every sector of society today.

A startling irony is that the very encounter people hunger for has become commodified as *time* and, thus, further crowds a supermaterialistic world. Unless extreme materialistic values are reexamined and the justification of their deep-seated orthodoxy questioned, the life-transforming impact of leadership is not possible. For such an engagement to be possible, theological waters need to be reexamined and revised. It demands a plunge into an intimate, transforming process as demonstrated by the woman who rediscovers herself and, thus, discovers her life's mission.

The narrative of John 4 embodies a meaningful model of leadership appropriate for today. Jesus's dialogical model embodies the unity of yin and yang. This contrasts with the extremely modernistic, yangish leadership we most often see in practice. The term yangish is borrowed from Taoism and refers to masculine energy. This masculine quest of competition and expansionism is deeply embedded in leadership, the local church, and the missions that often divide the body of Christ. Locked into pursuing numerical growth and expansion as measurements for success, leaders need a dialogical encounter with Jesus at the well to recover their own wholeness. The process of wholeness requires a fusion of yin and yang. In fact, it is the perfect balance of Jesus's yinish vulnerability and yangish confrontation that produces the transformation of the woman and her town.

Jesus's strength in radically breaking down the walls of racism, sexism, classism, regionalism, and religion is displayed in a yinish manner of vulnerability. His vulnerability comes not from ego but from the depth of a living, inner well. Sadly, many Christian leaders exercise leadership from their wounded egos. Likewise, the congregation projects their ego-based image of leadership onto their leaders. The projected image of leadership is not in any way a vulnerable one, but rather an image of strength.

My yearning for genuine and honest dialogue in a culture of placation has drawn me repeatedly to this narrative. It is heartwarming to see how chronic "isms," both ancient and contemporary, can be broken down by vulnerability. As depicted in the dialogue between Jesus and the Samaritan woman, much of leadership involves assisting people to recover within themselves the image of God. Restoring the tainted self-image, as modeled by Jesus Christ at the well, requires robust humility, a quality that is lacking in both men and women in leadership positions today. Don't we all need liberation from the poisonous internalized voices we hear daily, which cause us to yearn for approval from authority figures and to seek to climb the ladder of the elusive American dream?

Here are the crucial steps toward a life-transforming dialogical encounter:

1. love yourself
2. love others for who they are
3. be genuine and authentic enough to confront barriers
4. engage in differences
5. experience the redeeming power of grace beyond belief

Leaders, regardless of gender, can easily be conformed to the competitive track of the fast lane. I hope we make a special effort to simply hang out at the well and engage in dialogue with people with whom we do not usually socialize. That is the first step of following Jesus, who came to us as a stranger but redeemed us all, being fully human and fully God. Leadership is a sacred calling that stretches the mind, heart, and soul when modeled after the crucified Jesus who meets us resurrected. For such a sacred vocation, the sisters of Asian American Women on Leadership (AAWOL) have been getting together to quench our spiritual thirst and to become a well for many other women in the desert. Organic encounters cannot be replaced by virtual ones. Also, it is crucial that AAWOL not alienate men for the sake of the well-being of Asian American women. Our understanding of women's health cannot be reduced to gender alone. Our health encompasses sustainability of all God's creation. In this regard, the holistic yinist concept seeks and deserves dialogue with feminists, ecofeminists, womanists, and *mujeristas* alike.

Cross-Cultural Mediation (Acts 6)

The more we run from conflict,
The more it masters us;
The more we try to avoid it,
The more it controls us.
The less we fear conflict,
The less it confuses us;
The less we deny our differences,
The less they divide us.
                    David W. Augsburger[1]

As long as humans walk the earth, there will be conflict. This condition is universal and yet culturally particular. Stories from the Acts of the Apostles demonstrate how acting from a third space, the liminal realm beyond the yin and yang, can provide a valuable force for mediating conflict.

My interest in examining the dynamics of conflict mediation arises from two concerns: (1) internal disputes within mainline denominations, and (2) the ongoing eruptions of violence in the major cities of North America.

My first concern grows out of witnessing the frequency of church disputes that end up in civil court. These litigations can bankrupt a church's financial resources and scatter the body of Christ, jeopardizing the church's public witness. My second concern stems

---

1. David Augsburger, *Conflict Mediation across Cultures* (Louisville, KY: Westminster John Knox Press, 1992), 229.

from the violence and unrest in many of our cities.² These conflicts stem from generations of racial, political, and economic turmoil. Though the violence of these events is often shocking, the outcomes too often lead only to the perpetuation of a cycle of conflict.

Gridlock in human dialogue is extremely costly. The attacks on September 11, 2001, manifested one of the worst instances of mass killing in contemporary American history. As hegemonic policies and their global impact deplete economic, ecological, and human resources, two prime symbols of American financial and military power were targeted and attacked without warning: the World Trade Center and the Pentagon. While hell was unleashed in New York and Washington, the world was glued to the television screen as if it were all a Hollywood movie. Skyscrapers, symbols of modernity, collapsed as cultic leaders carried out their apocalyptic mission in the name of religion. It was as if the gods were at war. From out of a beautiful blue sky, terror rained death on three thousand innocent people; the fallout was an emotional bombshell that fell not only on the victims' families but on the nation as a whole. Most haunting, the attackers perished along with their innocent victims, leaving no passageway for justice, answers, or closure. Amid the fear of the faceless war, however, the unyielding human spirit of our first responders—the firefighters, police, EMTs, and other workers at ground zero—reminded us of the relentless courage that shines in the midst of evil.

At the heart of this event lies an ancient conflict dressed in modern technology. On the surface, culture appears to change. At a deeper level, ancient conflicts still persist in the modern and postmodern eras. Likewise, the apostles in the Acts of the Apostles experience both mediated and mediating roles as the gospel of Jesus Christ collides with ancient Judaism in a radically Hellenizing world. Seen through the lens of conflict mediation, Acts provides insights into our contemporary, globalizing world.

Because of radical technological innovation, both domestic and international migration have reached their peaks. As revealed in

---

2. I was living in Los Angeles during the 1992 uprising and in Ohio during the Cincinnati uprisings in 2001.

the case of Hebraic Jews and the Hellenists, an immigrant community's differences in language, birthplace, and traditions can become sources of discrimination. The application of Acts to contemporary immigrant communities stands strong despite vast time and cultural differences between New Testament times and ours.

The immigrant community in the United States is my social location for this chapter. I have pastored and taught in immigrant churches in urban and suburban areas of Los Angeles and the Midwest for twenty years. I also have ten years of teaching experience in the academic discipline of missiology, which is multidisciplinary and multicultural in scope. As a Korean American woman, I often find myself on the periphery of both cultures as I move to and from Korean and American contexts. The nature of multiplicity often accompanies continual oscillation between life experiences in the realm of the either/or, neither/nor, in-between, and both/and. This constant journey exposes me to issues of raw power. Learning to accept the strength of this in-between state as an asset has liberated me to move beyond the false dichotomous view of perceiving power only from the perspective of either the powerful or the powerless.

Acts 6: Dealing Openly with Conflict

No one wants to be excluded or pushed to the periphery. It is fundamental human nature to yearn for social inclusion. Therefore, much of human social drama and conflict plays out like a roller coaster ride of inclusion and exclusion. The main thesis of this chapter is that dealing openly and wisely with conflict can reduce levels of violence. The implementation of effective conflict mediation depends on three key components: timing, the availability of the mediator, and the nature of the conflict. Though the conflict between the worldviews of the Hebrews and the Hellenists is not one to be glossed over, this chapter ultimately celebrates the power of conflict mediation. This is a power that vitalizes the mission of the church.

The conflict in Acts 6:1 arises around a basic human need: food. The nature of this conflict is concrete, making it much easier to mediate than the deeply embedded historic conflict between the Hebrews and Hellenists that is the result of unhealed memories resurfacing in Acts (see 6:1; 7:51–60; 15:1–2). In response to the conflict around daily food distribution, the apostles' immediate and open decision-making process works to mediate the situation. They gather the disciples together and select seven Hellenists based on their wisdom and their fullness of Spirit. These seven are tasked with waiting on the tables of the Hellenist widows. This process is notable for its integrity and transparency. An ongoing sign of vitality in Christian churches is the capacity to deal with conflict openly and immediately across cultures.

Regrettably, in many churches today, conflict brews under the surface. This subterranean hostility either paralyzes or splits the body of Christ. The initial exclusion of the Hellenist widows from the daily food distribution uncovers the preexisting, but subterranean, tension between the Hebraic Jews and the Jewish diaspora in a rapidly Hellenizing world. Thus, it has a significant parallel to today's rapidly globalizing world. In the twenty-first century, we still face ancient and universal group dynamics centered on exclusion and domination, a politicized reaction to shifting power dynamics as minority groups challenge the way the pie is cut.

Growing Pains and Intergroup Conflict

Having experienced direct persecution in Acts 5, the apostles are confronted with an intergroup conflict in Acts 6. The apostles are confronted with their own group's exclusion of Grecian Jewish widows during daily food distribution. Only four chapters after the Spirit brings about unity in diversity at Pentecost, Luke records this division in the community. Tension between Greek and Hebraic Jews reaches its peak. According to James D. G. Dunn, the timing of the confrontation by the Hellenists is telling. As the number of Hellenist disciples grows, the Hellenists grumble against the Hebrews (6:1).[3] Empowered by this numerical growth, the Hellenists address their widows' complaint against the Hebraic Jews' unjust treatment. For the Hebraic Jews, the increasing number

---

3. James D. G. Dunn, *The Partings of the Ways: Between Christianity and Judaism and Their Significance for the Character of Christianity* (Valley Forge, PA: Trinity Press International, 1991), 61.

of Hellenists may have meant a drying up of the welfare system. An economic downtime sharpens existing differences and elevates competitiveness, while minimizing the value of mercy. In a tightly knit group, the distribution of limited goods favors the "in" group and thus marginalizes the "other." The Hellenists are unfortunately treated as outsiders in their own homeland after returning from their diaspora experience. This experience is paralleled today in the idealization of the homeland among immigrants, an idealization that is shattered when facing the contrasting realities of change within individual immigrants and within their homeland.

Heightened Otherness during Cultural Change

The backdrop for the events of Acts 6 is the larger issue of cultural change and its persistence in Judaism's encounters with Hellenism. Scholars vary in their views regarding Judaism and Hellenism. The most common description of Hellenists is that they were Jews born outside of Palestine but living in Jerusalem. These were Greek-speaking, not Aramaic-speaking, Jews. Shaye J. D. Cohen, however, asserts that Hellenistic culture comprised many different ethnic groups who expressed themselves in the Greek language and thus contained multiple elements. In other words, Hellenistic culture was a melting pot.

> The natives were Hellenized, and the Greeks were "Orientalized." Through intermarriage with local women and through veneration of the local gods, the Greeks often lost much of their Greekness. . . . In this conception, "Judaism" and "Hellenism" are not antonyms, since, by definition, Judaism was part of Hellenism and Hellenism was part of Judaism.[4]

Cohen argues against the antithetical dynamic between Judaism and Hellenism. Opposing the notion of a "pure" form of Judaism, he asserts that the land of Palestine was not a cultural island. As in today's globalizing world, the forces of sweeping cultural change

---

4. Shaye J. D. Cohen, *From the Maccabees to the Mishnah* (Philadelphia: Westminster Press, 1987), 36.

could not keep any culture from the dominant, in this case Hellenistic, influence. The notion that one group remains fixed against the tidal wave of a Hellenizing world is problematic in drawing distinctions between Hebraic Jews and diaspora Jews. Instead, "Hellenistic Judaism is only a chronological indicator for the period from Alexander the Great to the Maccabees or perhaps to the Roman conquests of the first century BCE."[5]

Furthermore, as Martin Hengel points out, Jerusalem was "not only a Jewish but also a 'Hellenistic' capital—surely sui generis— with its own Jewish Hellenistic culture." Greek-speaking Jews of the diaspora introduced synagogues in Jerusalem with the Pharisees' support.[6] Hengel describes Hellenists in Jerusalem as follows:

> This special Jewish-Hellenistic milieu in Jerusalem and its environment was formed by the Jewish pilgrims, returning emigrants and students of the law from the Greek-speaking Diaspora, by the members of the Herodian court, Herod's family and their clientele, by some aristocratic priestly families like the Boethusians, by merchants, physicians, architects and other technical specialists, teachers of Greek language and rhetoric, skilled artisans and also slaves from abroad. . . . From this Greek-speaking group came the Seven Hellenists in Acts 6, people like Joseph Barnabas, John Mark, Silas-Silvanus, and above all, Saulus-Paulus from Tarsus.[7]

The diversity of class among the Hellenists in Jerusalem is noteworthy. In addition to their intergroup conflict with Hebrew Jews, an intragroup conflict centers on class consciousness. The diaspora Jews from Asian Minor journeyed to Jerusalem and brought with them syncretized customs and religions. This raised a question among the Hebraic Jews as to how far Judaism ought to adapt to Hellenism. The responses, of course, varied. Some took an all-or-

---

5. Ibid.

6. Martin Hengel, "Judaism and Hellenism Revisited," in *Hellenism in the Land of Israel*, ed. John J. Collins and Gregory E. Sterling (Notre Dame, IN: University of Notre Dame Press, 2001), 26.

7. Ibid., 28.

nothing approach, and others took a partial adaptation position. Whereas some were prepared to relinquish all beliefs and practices, others had a merely rhetorical anti-Hellenistic stance. All such stances threatened the stability of Judaism.[8] As in today's globalized world, an unavoidable question that Jewish people confronted was centered on the issue of identity. How do Jews maintain Jewishness in a dominant Hellenistic culture? What is nonnegotiable and what is negotiable in such a changing world?

In this tumultuous time, the Pharisees played a stabilizing role. In contrast to the common portrayal of Pharisees as rigid legalists, many scholars now believe that the Pharisees supported a new system, with the synagogue providing space and structure for both Hebrew and Hellenist Jews. Nevertheless, tension around particulars and universals had to be overwhelming.

Responding to this tension, the synagogue structure utilized an integrationist approach, whereas the apostles utilized a cultural-pluralistic-resolution model by creating a deacon structure to handle the exclusion of the Hellenist widows. The apostles impressively drew clear role boundaries and offered a proposal that satisfied the whole group. They did not defend the Hebraic Jews nor blame the Hellenists. They listened to the problem and delegated the resolution to the insiders. Unlike Gamaliel's mediation, which utilized his fellow high priests to rescue the apostles in danger (5:33–40), in dealing with the Grecian widows, the apostles chose the wounded group, the Hellenists, to mediate. As the apostles presented their proposal, they made their communication channels and procedures clear and open. They provided leadership by presenting their proposal rather than leaving it to the masses, and then they delegated their leadership authority.

Often, conflict in the church snowballs because leaders either take total control or choose a rudderless, laissez-faire approach. The apostles' procedure was first to gather all the disciples together and stress their primary role as apostles—ministers of the word of God (6:2). Second, they presented a proposal to delegate to the congregation the resolution of the problem: "Friends, select from among yourselves seven men of good standing, full of the Spirit and

---

8. Cohen, *From the Maccabees to the Mishnah*, 45.

of wisdom, whom we may appoint to this task" (6:3). Third, the proposal satisfied the whole group (6:5). It appears that the seven chosen men became official mediators for the proposed problem. This was followed by rituals that granted authority to the seven men through prayer and the laying on of hands (6:6).

Such differences in styles of mediation stem from the nature of the conflict. In the former conflict between the apostles and the high priest in Acts 5, a core belief is threatened, while the conflict between the Hebraists and the Hellenists in Acts 6 involves negligent discriminatory behavior. Mediating chronic clashes in worldview cannot be resolved once and for all. They keep resurfacing throughout Acts and in the history of Christianity. The new wine bursts the old wineskin. In fact, the chosen key leader of the seven, Stephen, who mediates for Greek widows (6:8, 15), is stoned to death because he challenges "old wineskins." The conflict between the apostles and the high priests resurfaces, despite Gamaliel's temporary mediation; and it resurfaces again with a global impact as we confront ancient conflicts today in the Middle East.

Although critiquing ancient narratives from contemporary perspectives requires caution, I want to address some modern implications for the sake of today's reader. Whereas the apostles deserve admiration for freeing themselves from having to exercise power over the victim, a lingering question relates to this effective yet separatist solution to the problem. Does it reinforce a social and cultural distance by treating the poorest as the utterly other? It is often the powerful who can afford to draw clear-cut role boundaries while the lives of the poor, represented in the Greek widows' daily lives, revolve around simultaneous, multiple tasks. Especially in earlier centuries, gendered time and space categories placed women in polychronic time in contrast to the more male monochronic time. Women's tasks were many and varied, while men were allowed the luxury of focusing on just one task at a time.[9]

---

9. Young Lee Hertig, "Without a Face: The Nineteenth-Century Bible Woman and Twentieth-Century Female Jeondosa," in *Gospel Bearers, Gender Barriers: Missionary Women in the Twentieth Century*, ed. Dana L. Robert (Maryknoll, NY: Orbis Books, 2002), 185–99, at 193.

While such boundaries diffuse control, they also maintain social distance between the two conflicting groups. Although there is merit in delegating the job to the in-group members (Hellenist Jews), bridging the social distance cannot be achieved indirectly. The otherness defined by language, place of birth, migration, and emigration remains pronounced when a separatist rather than an integrationist approach is taken. Upon highlighting the guidelines of selecting leaders, the apostles draw clear role boundaries. They stress that "it is not right that we should neglect the ministry of the word of God in order to wait on tables" (6:2).

What happens if the apostles do not delegate moral responsibility? If they take a dialectic approach, they may potentially organize a joint task force. From an experiential perspective, the experience gap between the two groups appears to persist despite the numerical growth of believers: "The number of the disciples increased greatly in Jerusalem, and a great many of the priests became obedient to the faith" (6:7). There is no mention as to how the treatment of the cultural other improves. Greek widows, after their complaint, remain silent in the text. The proposed problem has to do with the Greek widows, and yet it ends with addressing the triumphant numerical growth of believers, including priests. One of the implications is that the proposed problem is resolved, and the end result is the expansion of Christianity, which then snowballs into a threat to the high priests and the martyrdom of Stephen, one of the seven Hellenist leaders.

The cost of an impasse in a conflict is enormous. In today's world, it results in massive ecological, human, and financial destruction. The impact of heightened conflict lasts generation after generation. When it increases, conflict brews to a boiling point and results in violent eruptions. Therefore, dealing with conflict openly and in an orderly way is significant, as demonstrated by the apostles and the Hellenists. The Hellenists' strategic moment of raising an issue "when the disciples were increasing in number" (6:1) is significant in dealing with discrimination. Much of politics revolves around engineering issues, timing, and accessing the right channels. Such discernment takes seasoned and wise leadership. Obviously, until the Hellenists bring up their widow's experience of injustice, they must have exercised silence. In such a case, not acting may serve as an active process, not an escape from conflict.

Hebraic Suspicion of Hellenized Jews

The numerical growth of a minority group sharpens group consciousness and thus results in intergroup tension, particularly when resources are limited. The dominant group believes that their piece of the pie is shrinking; but the minority believes that they deserve a fair share of the pie. Thus, justice and mercy are in conflict because of differing competitive values and perceptions of the way the pie is distributed. Lee G. Bolman and Terrence E. Deal indicate the conditions under which such conflict arose:

> The political frame asserts that in the face of enduring differences and scarce resources, conflict is inevitable and power is a key resource. Scarce resources force trade-offs. Enduring differences ensure that parties will disagree on both what and how to decide.[10]

Economic downtimes fuel existing conflicts, splitting scarce resources. In Acts, Luke exposes the intergroup conflict that marginalizes one group over another. In this case, the Hellenist widows in the Hellenizing world become "other." These widows then become the embodiment of otherness. As Miroslav Volf defines it, they are "those who are oppressed and in need of liberation."[11]

The sources of conflict can be traced back to the rift between the Hebraists and Hellenists, beginning with the Hellenistic reform in Jerusalem (175–164 BCE) when the Jewish Hellenists attempted to "convert Jerusalem to a 'Greek' city."[12] This event sent shockwaves

---

10. Lee G. Bolman and Terrence E. Deal, *Reframing Organizations: Ancestry, Choice, and Leadership* (San Francisco: Jossey-Bass Publishers, 1997), 164.

11. Miroslav Volf, "Exclusion and Embrace: Theological Reflections in the Wake of Ethnic Cleansing," *Journal of Ecumenical Studies* 29, no. 2 (Spring 1992): 235.

12. Hengel, "Judaism and Hellenism Revisited," 17. The key leadership of the revolt stemmed from the assimilation of the upper class and concluded with the apostasy of a smaller splinter group led by Menelaus.

through Palestinian Judaism during the Second Temple era. Hengel concludes that this radical reform ended as a failed attempt against "theocracy." It ideologically sought resistance by the majority of the Jewish people to pursue a violent break with ancestral law.[13] It resulted in the collapse of the Jewish internal system of authority, loyalty, and leadership because of the external pressures of Hellenization, which forced Judaism to adapt.

Dunn interprets Acts 6 in light of the "residue of suspicion" by devout Torah Jews toward Hellenist Jews from the time of the Maccabean revolt. The Maccabean revolt shook the core belief system of the Hebraic Jews as the Hellenizers challenged circumcision, food laws, and even the Temple sacrifices.[14] Consequently, Judea underwent a major paradigm shift due to Hellenization, which turned a cohesively unified society into a complex one. Judea's ideology was no longer representative as it clashed with the "new wineskins" initiated by Hellenism.

As in any revolutionary time, response to the external forces of change emerges and is expressed in at least one of three ways: all or nothing, in between, and both/and. Diverse responses inevitably accompany a power struggle within and without. Jewish history professor Ellis Rivkin offers an important insight regarding the internal conditions for such a revolution to occur:

> Revolutions do not occur gratuitously. They are set in motion by a pattern of change; they are not mechanically induced by any single thought or a single event. Revolutions can occur only when the processes of change have altered the perceptions of those who are experiencing the impact and pressure.[15]

In other words, revolution is dependent on many external pieces that are much bigger than the revolution itself. Internal differences in responding to the Hellenism forced on the Jews by Antiochus IV

---

13. Ibid., 19.
14. James D. G. Dunn. *The Acts of the Apostles* (Valley Forge, PA: Trinity Press International, 1996), 82.
15. Ellis Rivkin, *A Hidden Revolution* (Nashville, TN: Abingdon Press, 1978), 211–12.

(175–163 BCE) diffused structural cohesiveness; this in turn altered the old structure. This alteration was possible because there were enough in the elite class who were restless and frustrated by absolute theocracy.

Dunn also attributes language differences to the tension between the Hebraic Jews and the diaspora Hellenists. One of the most visible signs in intercultural contact is the language gap, just when the tool of communication is needed most. The Hebrew Jews, who spoke Aramaic and had to learn the dominant Greek language, must have been irritated by Hellenists, who were monolingual.[16] The Hebraic Jews had reason to be suspicious of people from the Hellenized diaspora and to perceive them as diluting the Hebrew core belief system.

The intense conflict between the Hebraists and the returning immigrants, the Hellenists, call to mind a similar dynamic occurring among immigrant communities today. The first generation's struggle to hold on to its indigenous belief system and the second generation's reaction against their parents in favor of assimilation to American culture evoke strong emotions in both generations. The conflict between the two groups mirrors current broader struggles related to race, ethnicity, gender, and religion.

The Challenge of Preserving Hebrew Identity

Amid such epochal change, the core beliefs of the Hebrews were challenged from every direction. Noted scholar on diaspora Judaism A. T. Kraabel writes, "The need for community in a bewildering larger world affected people at nearly every level of wealth and education. Jews began to form their own communities in the Greco-Roman world early in the Hellenistic period."[17]

In such challenging times, the conflict caused by the visible "otherness" undoubtedly escalates more than the greater "common-

---

16. Dunn, *Acts of the Apostles*, 81.
17. A. T. Kraabel, "Unity and Diversity among Diaspora Synagogues," in *Diaspora Jews and Judaism: Essays in Honor of, and in Dialogue with, A. Thomas Kraabel,* ed. J. Andrew Overman and Robert S. MacLennan (Atlanta: Scholars Press, 1992), 25.

ness." Ethnicity, nativism, and diaspora become sources of conflict, pitting one group against the other. Naturally, the Hebrews sought to hold back the tidal wave of sweeping Hellenization. In such a closed climate, the diaspora Jews in Jerusalem became an easy target for suspicion. Suspicion of the "other" led to their exclusion from the daily supplies needed for survival. Turning a fundamental need into a tool of discrimination instigates an emotional uproar from the excluded. In a potentially explosive situation, the apostles, in the wake of their conflict with the high priests, handle the case wisely.

Role Reversal: The Mediated Mediate

A role reversal takes place in Acts 6, where the mediated become the mediators. The apostles had gone through near-death experiences and been freed by Gamaliel's intervention in Acts 5. (Their success in preaching the gospel of Jesus had threatened the high priest and endangered their lives.) Now the freed apostles themselves face an opportunity to release the oppressed through their mediation. As we noted earlier in this chapter, however, unlike the direct mediation Gamaliel demonstrated, the apostles choose to delegate mediation to the "other," the Hellenists. They emphasized the boundaries of their role as apostles: "It is not right that we should neglect the word of God in order to wait on tables" (6:2); then they provided criteria for choosing Hellenists to handle the problem created by the Hebraic Jews: "Therefore, friends, select from among yourselves seven men of good standing, full of the Spirit and of wisdom, whom we may appoint to this task" (6:3). We can see two different kinds of mediation taking place in Acts 5 and Acts 6. The nature of conflict seems to determine the style of mediation, although the qualifications of the mediator remain the same.

Because of conflicting perceptions and experiences tainting realities, creating consensus in conflicting situations can be a challenge. The apostles' immediate and open consultation serves as an effective mediation. Often when conflict causes gridlock in an organization, communication is secretive and indirect. Conflict swept under the rug festers and increases. From the apostles' response, we can observe a very important process of conflict mediation:

1. They listened to the voices from the margins.
2. They drew healthy role differentiation.
3. They laid out open and clear guidelines for selecting leaders.
4. They delegated power to the Greek Jews without strings attached.
5. Spirit-filled leaders, such as Stephen and Philip, were chosen for the new leadership team.
6. They legitimized chosen leaders through public authorization.

The apostles' process is exemplary. They do not show signs of needing to control the situation. Although not selected by the apostles themselves, the seven leaders whom the apostles install into office successfully meet their criteria. And if the delegation had been carried out blindly and carelessly, it would have intensified conflict rather than reduced it. Although the task force deals with one concrete issue successfully, the fundamental identity conflict remains unresolved, as indicated by Stephen's death. While key leaders, like Stephen, are byproducts of Pentecost, the widening gap between core Jewish identity and the gospel of Jesus Christ persists. For this reason, I prefer the term conflict mediation, not conflict resolution, in approaching complex human dynamics. Yesterday's hasty resolution can revisit as today's nightmare.

Pentecost as Source of Both Unity and Division

Pentecost transcends linguistic barriers through the miraculous work of the Holy Spirit (Acts 2). Everyone understands the others. The Holy Spirit miraculously bridges linguistic, regional, and ethnic differences. After Pentecost, the believers are "of one heart and soul," and "everything they owned was held in common" (Acts 4:32). Barriers of otherness no longer matter, and reciprocity creates a powerful community.

The powerful intervention of the unifying Holy Spirit, however, is marred by persistent human discord. Human boundaries rooted in difference and otherness quickly resurface, as in the story of

Ananias and Sapphira. The couple bears false witness to the Holy Spirit by concealing parts of the proceeds of their land. Confronted by Peter, they drop dead on the spot, creating fear among the believers. The signs and wonders that were once sources of unity now become sources of tension between the Sanhedrin and the apostles. At Pentecost, the Holy Spirit brings about a reconciliation of differences that challenge the status quo. The conflict rises to the high priest and associates. Ultimately, a party of Sadducees arrests the apostles, but in vain. The high priest declares, "We gave you strict orders not to teach in this name, yet here you have filled Jerusalem with your teaching and you are determined to bring this man's blood on us" (5:8). But Peter and the apostles reply, "We must obey God rather than any human authority" (5:29).

Gamaliel's Mediation

Although Peter's level of defiance corresponds to the level of oppression by the high priest, his outright defiance against the high priest's authority worsens the conflict. Both the message and the messenger paralyze any dialogue. Meeting confrontation with confrontation cannot ease tension. Edward DeBono accurately stresses, "Disputants are in the worst position to solve their disputes."[18] It requires a third-party neutral mediator, one who is Spirit-filled and honored. Often the mediation hinges on the availability of such a mediator at the peak of tension. Gamaliel stands up during the peak of conflict and powerfully diffuses the heightened emotion:

> So in the present case, I tell you, keep away from these men and let them alone; because if this plan or this undertaking is of human origin, it will fail; but if it is of God, you will not be able to overthrow them—in that case you may even be found fighting against God! (Acts 5:38–39)

A key quality of the mediator is shown in Gamaliel, who is respected—honored—by all the people (5:34). Bruce J. Malina and Jerome H. Neyrey differentiate ascribed honor and achieved honor

---

18. Edward DeBono, *Conflicts* (London: Harrap, 1985), 92.

in the Mediterranean world. Ascribed honor is more highly valued, whereas acquired honor occurs "in virtue of performance" and thus opens up room for challenge by the other performer.[19] His status granted, Gamaliel possesses both ascribed honor as an insider and achieved honor through his powerful speech. As an insider putting on the outsider's perspective, he rescues the apostles from being put to death. His seasoned character diffuses rigidly bound perceived threats in need of a reality check. Successfully modeling mediation, Gamaliel diffuses the high priest's charge after the defendant, Peter, aggravates the tension with his direct response. Thus, the role of mediator in changing antagonistic perceptions is crucial in intergroup conflict mediation because everyone sees reality through his or her own tinted glasses.

Several key principles emerge for the role of mediator from Gamaliel's example of using his powerful position to empower the powerless:

- He utilized both ascribed and achieved honor.
- He utilized both emic (insider) and etic (outsider) perspectives on the conflict.
- He expanded the dichotomous either/or perception to a reciprocal both/and perception.
- He wisely transported the insider's fixed perception toward the higher purposes of God.

Missiologically, it is important to note that once conflict is mediated it accompanies the vitality of the mission of the church. After Gamaliel resolves the conflict, Acts 5:42 states that "every day in the temple and at home they did not cease to teach and proclaim Jesus as the Messiah." Likewise, when the conflict about the Hellenist widows is resolved through the appointment of Hellenist leaders, Luke again describes the vitality of the church: "The word of God continued to spread; the number of the disciples increased

---

19. Bruce J. Malina and Jerome H. Neyrey, "Honor and Shame in Luke-Acts: Pivotal Values of the Mediterranean World," *in The Social World of Luke-Acts*, ed. Jerome H. Neyrey (Peabody, MA: Hendrickson Publishers, 1991), 25–65, at 47.

greatly in Jerusalem, and a great many of the priests became obedient to the faith" (6:7). The exclusion of Hellenist widows is unjust; so vitality and justice issues are linked.

Unfortunately, the ideal community of sharing and growth originating at Pentecost comes and goes in the narrative. Barriers based on region, ethnicity, and language, though temporarily mediated, continue to resurface throughout Acts.

The Contemporary Emergence of Conflict

A tumultuous conflict results when ideals, rules, roles, and relationships no longer hold together. As in biblical times, conflict between groups in contemporary times emerges when minority groups' numbers increase. Racial tension in the major cities of the United States escalates as the majority group encounters increasing numbers of minority groups. For example, Los Angeles periodically experiences violence stemming from racialized policies in multicultural contexts. As in many political dynamics, discerning the right timing of raising the issues and the right representatives determines the outcome of the conflict. We will now examine the implications of Acts 6 in light of contemporary cultural conflict.

Implications for the Immigrant Church Today

Many immigrant churches today suffer from chronic conflict and a crisis of leadership. In fact, many leaders are embroiled in existing church conflict and are breeding emergent conflict. A significant area of conflict within the immigrant church includes differences between and within generations in worship, polity, personnel, and decision-making procedures. Often, language barriers for the first generation limit their social boundaries. Consequently, the immigrant church becomes the primary social milieu where members bring all of their unmet social needs. The American-born second generation wants to worship God according to their own preferences rather than simply mimicking their parents' model; the parents want to make sure their traditions continue through their offspring.

In the absence of shared decision-making criteria and leadership like that exemplified by Stephen and Gamaliel, the contemporary immigrant church often creates social chaos. Increasingly, church matters are brought to litigation, which taxes the church's resources and lowers the quality of the church. Therefore, the role of tradition in the immigrant community is entrenched and becomes stronger than that of the mainstream culture that was left behind; that is, cultural change takes place faster in the mainstream culture than on the "island" subculture of immigrants. For many immigrants, tradition offers continuity in the midst of disruptive changes. Because of these surrounding changes, immigrants can easily cling to tradition—denominational, cultural, or familial—like a security blanket.[20]

The ongoing spiritual vitality of the immigrant church challenges leaders to be equipped for mediation and peacemaking. Trained in a highly monocultural seminary curriculum, many younger generation leaders graduate, return to the immigrant church with the same lack of indigenous leadership models, and then repeat the first generation's leadership style, which they had vehemently resisted. Thus, the perpetuation of dysfunctional leadership rather than adoption of contextual leadership is transmitted to the younger generation. Who can serve as a healthy third party for handling the immigrant church's clash of worldviews?

Perhaps theological education is the key to such a breakthrough. A change from a theological education dominated by Western thought would enhance both Western and non-Western theological education. It is time we practice reciprocity and mutuality—like the apostles who provided an opportunity for the "others" to represent their own group—in the theological enterprise and thus in ministry. Despite the current self-critique of the Christendom model of theological education, implementing an alternative will remain bleak until non-Western leaders come to the table.[21]

---

20. Young Lee Hertig, *Cultural Tug of War: The Korean Immigrant Family and Church in Transition* (Nashville, TN: Abingdon Press, 2001), 93.

21. Douglas John Hall's *The End of Christendom and the Future of Christianity* (Valley Forge, PA: Trinity Press International, 1997) is one book in a series entitled *The Christian Mission and Modern Culture* that gives a critique of Christendom.

If the seventeenth-century Enlightenment has contributed to the theological paradigm of the West and has had a global impact, then today's multicultural paradigms may contribute to charting out a theological discourse for the twenty-first century that moves beyond mere discussions about multiculturalism, mutuality, and reciprocity. Based on Acts 5 and 6, the either/or epistemology that fosters conflict can be reduced by adopting a both/and epistemology. It is time for the American immigrant church to exercise ownership of relevant paradigms without denigrating the West or idealizing its own paradigm, but rather balancing the Western extreme with newer paradigms through partnership for the sake of mutuality and reciprocity. Such a paradigm will allow differences to enrich all groups.

While some post-9/11 responses have cast fear and doubt on the value of human diversity, the apostles provide an inspiring and viable model through their willingness to offer the Hellenists a voice as well as structural support. The apostles' approach to conflict mediation contributes wisdom, justice, and mission vitality. Acts 6 clearly demonstrates the link between missional vitality and mediating conflict in the midst of diversity and immigration.

Becoming the Body of Christ (1 Corinthians 12)

The Body as a Unit

Both Jesus and the apostle Paul describe Christian identity and unity in holistic terms, as a living and undivided body. As Fritjof Capra notes, the term "holistic," from the Greek *holos* ("whole"), refers to an "understanding of reality in terms of integrated wholes whose properties cannot be reduced to those of smaller units."[1] This integrated wholeness also parallels the psychological concepts of gestalt and systems theory. For Jesus, wholeness is demonstrated as he offers his body as a sacrificial Lamb on the evening of the Passover. In his words, "Take it; this is my body. . . . This is my blood of the covenant, which is poured out for many" (Mark 14:22, 24). Jesus lays himself down in order for us to be whole, setting a radical contrast to the culture of hegemony and self-service. By yielding one's own life for the sake of the greater whole, this paradoxical wholeness characterizes a yinist concept of unity.

The apostle Paul's metaphor of becoming the body of Christ, in contrast to reductionistic Cartesian thought, elucidates the unity among the parts and the integrated whole. Furthermore, for separate parts to become a single body, the weaker parts warrant preferential treatment for the sake of balance:

---

1. Fritjof Capra, *The Turning Point: Science, Society, and the Rising Culture* (Toronto: Bantam Books, 1983), 38.

those parts of the body that seem to be weaker are indispensable, and the parts that we think are less honorable we treat with special honor. And the parts that are unpresentable are treated with special modesty, while our presentable parts need no special treatment. (1 Corinthians 12:22–24)

Many churches today face the challenges and opportunities of diversity but often remain mutually broken rather than integrated. Because I have seen the broken pieces of many churches, Paul's ecclesiology of the body of Christ has captivated me. According to Chinese medicine, illness stems from imbalance. Likewise, churches cease to be the body of Christ when the majority of congregants, that is, women, do not hear from women preachers. Androcentric pulpits bar women preachers. As a result, many capable Asian Pacific Islander (API) women leaders opt out of API churches to join Caucasian congregations where they can live out their calling and full gifts for the body of Christ. Sadly, API women are faced with this zero-sum scenario. Their longing for gender equality has to trump their ethnicity in order to fulfill their calling.

Oblivious to the stained-glass ceiling of API women leaders, API churches at large perpetuate their broken androcentric pulpit in the name of God. Recently, a young API woman candidate for a youth pastor position in Southern California was turned down when she shared that she was an egalitarian. Even at my age, I continue to experience gender disparity. In July of 2018, during a visit to a local API immigrant church, I had an encounter that might be almost humorous if not for its incivility. Immediately after Sunday worship, a greeting line was formed at the sanctuary doors to receive worshipers as they exited the sanctuary. This line consisted of three men: the guest preacher, the lead pastor, and a male elder. Because I was there to set up an appointment with the lead pastor for a project, I happened to stand near this all-male greeting line. It had been a while since I entered a Korean immigrant church's space on a Sunday. It felt strange to witness the endless bowings. As I waited for an opportunity to speak with the lead pastor, an usher rushed up to accost me and have me step away from the patriarchs. Obviously, it must have been a taboo for a woman to appear to stand in the greeting line. The question did cross my mind whether the usher would have bowed to me if I handed him my "Reverend Dr." business card. Would my gender trump my titles?

Contrary to the rules of what constitutes the body of Christ, patriarchal culture persists in API churches. In fact, the reversal of affirmative action is normative. The powerful parts receive respect while the weaker parts receive disrespect. Yet, they still call themselves the body of Christ when the weaker parts are invisible and dismissed. The alienation of certain parts jeopardizes the wholeness of the body, a wholeness that requires all parts to become one. Paul, however, stresses having equal concern for one another:

> But God has combined the members of the body and has given greater honor to the parts that lacked it, so that there should be no division in the body, but that its parts should have equal concern for each other. (1 Corinthians 12:24–25)

The rubric of becoming the body of Christ diametrically opposes the capitalistic culture that pervades all systems. Churches are no exception, as they seek numbers, dollars, and buildings for expansion, all of which are regarded as markers of success, just as in the corporate world. In this milieu, often the weaker, who lack a protective power base, fall prey to the stronger. Giving greater honor to the parts that lack it and having equal concerns in our world's record-breaking inequality mean, then, relinquishing the capitalistic worldview of *money-begets-money* and becoming prophetic and countercultural. Practicing the worldviews of interdependency, not fragmentation, and mutual particularity, not conformity, are the keys to becoming the body of Christ. Mutual particularity affirms the otherness of each part and embodies togetherness.

The Constantinization of Christianity shifted a resistant spirit under persecution to an ambitious spirit of expansionism. Consequently, the prophetic voice has waned, and the megachurch phenomenon has dominated the Protestant church. The program-driven expansionism of the church not only exhausts pastoral leaders but also economic resources. The desire to launch franchised churches sets up a quasi-papal Protestant system: the founder preaches on the main campus, and then on the satellite campuses, the gathered body of Christ becomes spectators of the digital spectacle on giant screens. It feels as though the clock has turned back to the pre-Reformation era.

Unity of Mind, Body, and Spirit

In the last two decades, neuroscience has finally begun to validate the Eastern holistic approach to human health and well-being. In her bestselling book *Women's Bodies, Women's Wisdom,* Christiane Northrup confirms ancient healing traditions:

> The mind and the body are intimately linked via the immune, endocrine, central nervous, and connective tissue systems. Today, mind–body research is confirming what ancient healing traditions have always known: that the body and the mind are a unity. There is no disease that isn't mental and emotional as well as physical.[2]

Quantum physics, according to Northrup, informs us that "at the subatomic level, matter and energy—called spirit—are interchangeable. Contrary to the notion that thoughts, emotions, and the brain are separate, neuroscience confirms that they are all connected within one system and thus '*the mind is located throughout the body*' and even beyond."[3] The verification of the interconnectedness of our bodies, minds, and spirits is revolutionary to Westerners like Northrup. The seamless unity of our entire body counters the patriarchal epistemology but corresponds to what Paul elaborated in 1 Corinthians 12. As Northrup observes,

> Most modern civilizations are characterized by the belief that the intellect is superior to emotions, the mind and spirit are

---

2. Christiane Northrup, *Women's Bodies, Women's Wisdom: Creating Physical and Emotional Health and Healing,* rev. and updated (New York: Bantam Books, 2010), 26.

3. Ibid., 32.

superior to and entirely separate from the body, and masculinity is superior to femininity.[4]

In overcoming this reductionistic Western mindset, the concept of *Tao Te Ching* can provide a more holistic way of being.

Tao Te Ching: Fusion of Faith and Action

An emphasis on theological knowledge (rather than practical theology) is transmitted through seminary education, where seminarians are discouraged from actively engaging in their social realities. Many pastors who have gone through theological education are crippled by the lack of holistic education. Tao Te Ching offers a theological model that connects mind, body, and spirit. In the concept of Tao Te Ching, there is no separation of theory from action. According to Lao Tzu, "Tao means the integral truth of the universe, Te means the virtuous application of such high, subtle knowledge, and Ching means serious spiritual guidance."[5] Therefore, Tao Te Ching reconciles the dichotomy of belief and action. Taoism as a paradigm can offer hope of recovering broken dimensions of humanity and nature, church and the world, other world and this world, and male and female.

When our lens is enlarged, we are able to see the whole picture, not just part of it. We can then view a kaleidoscope of beauty. Policies accompanied by a kaleidoscopic perspective will serve all segments of the society. The choice of yielding takes the strength of inner spirituality. Everyone must realize we are all beautiful parts in the design of a kaleidoscopic circle.

In the Eastern mind, the very essence of learning takes place when there is a fusion between the idea and being. The ancient wisdom of the "sageliness within and kingliness without" shines light on our contemporary quest for "kingliness without" that

---

4. Ibid., 4.

5. Hua-Ching Ni, trans., *The Complete Works of Lao Tzu: Tao Teh Ching & Hua Hu Ching* (Santa Monica, CA: Seven Star Communications, 1995), 3.

lacks "sageliness within."[6] In the discipline of the sage, ideas and deeds are one, and thus the Western quest for practical theology stemming from the dichotomy is not necessary.

Too often, the polarized representation of yin and yang around gender stereotypes impoverishes humanity and inflicts harm that otherwise could be the very source of human well-being. According to Taoism, it is the lack of balance—extreme polarity—that harms humans and the universe. The healthy human being cannot stand on the fragmented extreme of *either* the yang-based *or* the yin-based life.[7]

Northrup's notion of belief as physical also shares the similar concept of Tao Te Ching:

> Thoughts are an important part of our body's wisdom because we have the ability to change our minds (and our thoughts) as we learn and grow. A thought held long enough and repeated enough becomes a belief. The belief then becomes biology. Beliefs are vibrational forces that create the physical basis of our individual lives and our health.[8]

Therefore, working through self-destructive thoughts and subsequent feelings can prevent physical distress.

Embodiment

Author and journalist Chris Hedges invokes Søren Kierkegaard in lamenting that rational obstruction separates intellect from emotions, ourselves from others, and ourselves from the sacred, thus numbing the soul.[9] Meanwhile, Western minds are increasingly

---

6. Fung Yu-Lan, *A Short History of Chinese Philosophy: A Systematic Account of Chinese Thought from Its Origins to the Present Day*, ed. Derk Bodde (New York: Free Press, 1948), 8.

7. Young Lee Hertig, "The Asian-American Alternative to Feminism: A *Yinist* Paradigm," *Missiology: An International Review* 26, no. 1 (January 1998): 15–22, at 19–20.

8. Northrup, *Women's Bodies, Women's Wisdom*, 35.

9. Chris Hedges, "The Cost of Resistance," *Common Dreams*, November 2017, https://www.commondreams.org.

embracing Eastern thought as a quest for a more holistic paradigm. Neuroscience, for example, has been at the forefront in touting the promising benefits of acupuncture and other Eastern healing modalities that approach the body as an integrated whole.

My interest in Taoism is neither coincidental nor academic, but instead dates back to experiences in my early childhood. My grandfather was an acupuncturist and herbalist. Whenever I visited his home, I saw the human anatomy in full display with all the meridian points marked. Chinese medicine and acupuncture derive from Taoist concepts.

Jung Young Lee's numerous theological writings in dialogue with Taoism have helped me to conceptualize a yinist paradigm. He has provided footing for those who come after him to see Christianity through an Asian lens. His critique of an overly externalized Western Christianity compels him to emphasize the inner process, as he elaborates the wholeness of the body of Christ from a Taoist interdependency. Churches today could become more whole if they were to embrace Lee's theology of empathy.

Another theologian I rely on is Anselm Min, who has two PhDs—one in philosophy and the other in theology. His article on "solidarity of others" fits with Paul's ecclesiology of preferential treatment or affirmative action. Anselm Min's theological richness, with one foot in Western theological tradition and the other in Asian and Asian American locations, offers a possibility for translating "solidarity of others" into a yinist paradigm. Min's use of the postmodern term "other" can be linked to how to develop the body as a unit. The term "other" in the postmodern sense refers to:

> human beings in their dignity, a dignity that transcends and resists reduction to identity (subjective or collective) and, thus, resistance to theoretical and practical totalization. It intends a critique of domination defined by closed system of identity.[10]

---

10. For a definition of the "other" in the postmodern sense, see Anselm Kyongsuk Min, "Solidarity of Others in the Body of Christ: A New Theological Paradigm," *Toronto Journal of Theology* 14, no. 2 (1998): 244–45.

The term "other" also indicates "those excluded from social systems of identity; victims of such totalizing reduction, the economically exploited, politically oppressed, culturally deprived, the socially marginalized."[11] The "other," therefore, has to be attended to with special care if we are to become a unified body as a whole.

Although we Asian American women fit into the descriptions of "other," we remain too restless to settle for the term. While it is indeed dangerous to emphasize specific identities that do not integrate but separate, a particular identity for Asian American women has not even been named. How do you unify when the identity is not yet defined? We are invisible and nameless, while feminist, womanist, and *mujerista* traditions have marked their collective cultural identities. Our dignity as Asian American women cannot be realized until we understand our particularity.

A hidden people's identity needs to be named in order to enter into public discourse. I have therefore named the Asian American "other" as yinist. There is power in naming invisible and unrecognized pain so that it may be attended with special care. It is named yinist because in the faith community, it is yin aspects that have been underrepresented. However, highlighting yin does not exclude yang in a binary perspective but rather a duality in motion.

According to Harold Coward, the *I Ching*'s correlative thinking parallels what Carl Jung calls "synchronicity." For Western persons to grasp synchronicity, they must temporarily relinquish their "fixation" on rationality and causal thought. "Synchronicity" borrows from Taoism's key ideas of resonance and correlations. In contrast to the Western idea of cause and effect, Chinese thinking is embedded in "correlative thinking."[12]

Yinist Ecclesiology

This chapter seeks to highlight the underrepresented Asian American women's perspective by offering, at least, a name—yinist, taken from Taoism for its duality.

---

11. Ibid.

12. Harold Coward, "Taoism and Jung: Synchronicity and the Self," *Philosophy East & West* 46, no. 4 (October 1996): 477–95, at 478.

In translating an ancient paradigm into contemporary settings, one has to deal with multiple hermeneutical horizons that require historical and contemporary contextual analysis. Nevertheless, the beauty of a classic paradigm lies in the fact that its applicability transcends time and space. Within both modernity and postmodernity, yangish and yinish responses are present.

Because of the familiarity of the Western notion of "either/or," understanding the "both/and" concept can easily lead to misinterpretation. Such dialectical harmony is lacking in today's hypercapitalistic and hyperdigitalized environment. In larger measure, modern culture is saturated by profit, interest, competition, and the commodification of human life. "Kingliness without" dominates the environment—economic, political, religious, familial, and the individual.

Jung Young Lee pioneered ecclesiology from a Taoist epistemology. Differentiating two terms used for the church—*koinonia* and *ekklesia*—Lee diffuses the boundaries between the secular and the sacred. Stressing the dual aspects of ecclesiology, Lee writes, "the inner quality of the ekklesia is koinonia, which means the community of love. . . . The koinonia is then the inner essence of the ekklesia and the criterion of being the true Church."[13] The *koinonia* might then be referred to as yin and *ekklesia* as yang. However, in examining the inner dimension of the church, one finds that *koinonia* in light of the church as the body of Christ is significant. As Anselm Min stresses, *koinonia* does not mean fellowship among those who are alike. Rather, it means the fellowship of the "other," which embodies diversity in unity.[14]

Koinonia in the immigrant church lacks the dimension of a "solidarity of others." Instead, it tends to manifest a "solidarity of likeness." Such exclusive solidarity begets tribalism and tribalism begets friction; this friction results in litigation, and litigation splits the body of Christ, thus perpetuating a vicious cycle. The

13. Jung Young Lee, *The I: A Christian Concept of Man* (New York: Philosophical Library, 1971), 116.
14. Min, "Solidarity of Others," 245.

precursor of "solidarity of others" agrees with what Jung Young Lee advocates: an empathic inner processing. Lee states,

> Yin and yang, or negative and positive, are mutually inter-dependent and coexist because of empathy. Empathy is like the gravity which pulls all together toward the center of earth.[15]

Likewise, the "solidarity of others," the dialectic interdependence of *"particularity* and *togetherness,"* can be interwoven through an empathic inner process. Lee critiques the externalization of Christianity, which has become hollow.

> For so many years the essential teaching of Jesus has been buried within the external process of institutional, social and rational frameworks that it is difficult to accept its intrinsic significance. The need for a spiritual life seems to increase in our time, but Christianity has lost the capability to fulfill it. It has been externalized and has lost its inner reality, the essential teaching of Jesus. Without the essential teaching of Jesus, that is, the inner process, Christianity loses its authenticity and relevance to meet the spiritual need of men.[16]

I call this inner spirituality a yinist spirituality. It fosters Christian living from the inside out through *koinonia*, the fellowship of others. Fellowship within homogeneity is a tribal fellowship of likeness. The body of Christ, which the apostle Paul addresses, is a "solidarity of others" in which each part maintains particularity and yet connectedness to the body as a whole.[17] Such unity of the body of Christ requires a shifting of the existing paradigm of competition, external growth, and external value.

The inside/out process, which occurs through the unity of yin and yang within each individual, will reflect the unity of the body

---

15. Jung Young Lee, *Patterns of Inner Process: The Rediscovery of Jesus' Teachings in the I Ching and the Writings of Preston Harold* (Secaucus, NJ: Citadel Press, 1976), 174.

16. Ibid., 206.

17. Min, "Solidarity of Others," 239–54.

of Christ. The holistic duality of yin and yang offers a rich theological lens through which we can theologize and indigenize.

According to a yinist ecclesiology, there is no room for the immigrant church to remain a silent island in the face of injustice because it offers the duality of *koinonia* and *ekklesia*. Within the immigrant community, the most visible diverse fellowship comprises class difference. The fellowship of the rich and the poor, male and female, and the first and second generation within the immigrant church requires an empathic journey. The glue that can weave "others" into solidarity is the empathic inner process based on the universality of love.

Justice and love ought to characterize the core of church life (Micah 6:8). However, it is not just or loving when the church chooses to split rather than integrate; then the church ceases to be the body of Christ. Because the church growth movement and modernity have converged and have focused on the concept of church as exterior, we are confronted frequently with the fallout of extreme conformity in defining the church. As indicated in the summary of the Korean immigrant church with the three pillars of numbers, tithes, and buildings, this extreme version of "the bigger the better" as a value in church practice manifests dark sides that create friction, church splits, and litigation.

A yinist paradigm, as one of the primordial consciousnesses of Asian and Asian Americans, parallels the Pauline concept of wholeness in 1 Corinthians 12. It is an old, yet new, concept because it engages today's postmodern reality of interdependency.

Taoism offers an alternative paradigm that balances the extremely externalized faith and church. What I mean by balancing here is that inner centering allows the outer expression of social witness. One without the other is not authentic. The internalization of faith, yin, needs to precede the external expression of faith, yang, in the public arena. Lacking the yinish internalization of faith, and simultaneously feeling powerless over the naked public square, Korean immigrants usher their reactionary yangish expression into the church. Heavily reinforced by externally defined success, the Korean immigrant church devotes its energy on a whim on any and every program. Thus, the balancing of faith through both yin and yang aspects is crucial for any consciousness to emerge. It stresses the church's inward journey for outward witness. The yinist paradigm derived from Taoism reconciles a dualistic, fragmented understanding of the gospel and the church and integrates all parts of the body of Christ.

Indeed, if churches are to become the body of Christ, the painful disconnect between the feminine side of God and the church, and the church and the world, must be bridged. The whole is bigger than the sums of its parts. The healthy body of Christ means that each part is exercising his or her sacred gifts in connection with every other part of the body.

• PART THREE •

Contemporary Embodiments
of Yinist Spirituality

"If I Perish, I Perish"

Maria Kim and Yu Kwan Soon

From 1996 to 2000, several visits to Korea compelled me to investigate the stories of courageous early Korean Christian women pioneers. It saddened me to learn that their spirit of resistance, which could offer theological wholeness and anchoring to today's desensitized Korean churches, had left no trace in contemporary Korean Christianity. Under the sway of globalization, Korean society drifts along without serious resistance; yet, Korean history is marked by resilient resistance, having survived over four hundred foreign invasions.

Early Korean Christians provided crucial and sacrificial leadership in nonviolent resistance to Japanese colonization. Forgotten are the stories of powerful Christian women whose struggle against the imperial Japanese was pivotal in bringing about Korea's eventual independence. Among the many who gave their lives for the cause of Korean emancipation, two key leaders stand out: Maria Kim and Yu Kwan Soon. In their work of resistance against Japanese annexation, a dialectic truth of yin and yang is exemplified. Their fearless resistance (yang) against torture and violence was derived from their spirit of surrender to death (yin). The latter is exemplified by the words of Esther 4:16, "If I perish, I perish."

My own social and cultural contexts impact my interpretations of historical figures such as Maria Kim and Yu Kwan Soon. I am a woman. I am a native Korean, a Korean American, and an ordained Presbyterian minister; I am also bilingual, bicultural, and a scholar with both an insider's and an outsider's perspective in relating to Korea as well as North America. My academic discourse is interdisciplinary and utilizes a case-study methodology. I bring this complexity with me, a rich amalgamation of perspectives, as I approach my work.

My contention is that contemporary Korean society faces a new form of colonization that, though it is less overt and violent than a military occupation, is potentially equal in threat: coca-colonization.[1] This term refers to the global domination of mega-corporations, such as the term's namesake, Coca Cola, which hinders competition from small, indigenous entities. This commercial influence is paralleled on the theological front, where dominant Western theologies often prevent the development of native theologies. On the verge of wholesale seduction by coca-colonization, Korean society is faced with several insistent questions: What are the factors that render such a disconnection? Why is it crucial to revisit the tenacious spirit of Kim and Yu in the twenty-first century? What relevance do they have in today's world? Is our level of resistance dependent on the oppressor's level of brutality? In the absence of serious consciousness raising, we once again need to tap into the spirit of resistors such as Maria Kim and Yu Kwan Soon in order to rally against the readily available and seductive mammonization of Korea.

The type of colonization that Kim and Yu faced during the turn of the century differs from our challenges in the twenty-first century. The former faced a brutal military force, the latter a seductive commercial force. Yet, a call for resistance against such domination remains the same. The relentless Christian resistance of Maria Kim and Yu Kwan Soon has been regretfully discontinued due to a theology that is divorced from the material world and

---

1. This term was popularized by Reinhold Wagnleitner in *Coca-Colonization and the Cold War: The Cultural Mission of the United States in Austria after the Second World War* (Chapel Hill, NC: University of North Carolina Press, 1994).

instead focused on the otherworld. We have thus confined Korean Christianity within the walls of the sanctuary. Bridging the discontinued spirit of resistance to the contemporary landscape will provide theological identity to this current generation confronting coca-colonization. By reconnecting with our silenced historical consciousness, "the mass" (*daejung*) will be transformed into "the people" (*minjung*), empowering those who resist the culture of coca-colonization.

The Role of Christianity and the Korean Independence Movement

The dawn of the twentieth century was one of the most turbulent times in Korean history. After five hundred years, the Yi Dynasty was waning. An opportunistic Japan capitalized on this transitional moment to colonize the Korean peninsula. The Korean people demonstrated fierce nonviolent resistance against the overwhelmingly armed Japanese colonizers. One of the most remarkable examples of resistance in Korean history is the March First Independence Movement of 1919—known as "Sam-il" (3-1), denoting the March 1 date. This movement is particularly significant because it united the Korean people across religious and generational divides to work toward the common goal of freeing their motherland. Four major groups consolidated for the independence movement: Chundokyo, Christians, Christian student groups, and Buddhists.[2]

Several domestic and international events prompted the leaders of the March First Movement to act. Domestically, a comprehensive eight-year land survey was implemented in order to seize Korean farmlands, religious temples, shrines, and other properties. These properties were then transferred to Japanese settlers at low costs. Meanwhile, Korea's king, Kojong, died suddenly in an apparent Japanese assassination. The March First event occurred two days before Kojong's funeral.

---

2. Kyung Bae Min, *KidokKyo KyoHyeSa* (Korean Church History), (Seoul, Korea: Yonsei University Press, 1993), 340.

Approximately one year prior in the United States, President Woodrow Wilson put forth his Declaration of Self-Determination in January of 1918. This doctrine spread globally, including into the Korean Peninsula. In turn, Korean Christian leaders wrote a Korean version of the Declaration of Independence, which impassioned the resistance movement. The peace conference held in Paris in April 1919 became a focal point for Korean Christian leaders to draw international attention to the brutal atrocities of the Japanese imperial military.[3]

Frustrated with ailing Confucianism, Korean intellectuals turned to Christianity. They pursued Western education as a primary vehicle for social change. Christianity provided a new impetus for Korean people under the Japanese regime. Unlike in other Third World countries, Christianity came to Korea without the baggage of Western colonization. It was thus readily used as fuel for a resistance movement against the Japanese occupation. Inspired by biblical narratives, key leaders dedicated their lives to the emancipation of the motherland from the torture of the Japanese armed forces. The Korean Declaration of Independence was instrumental in mobilizing the people's nonviolent movement.

The Korean independence movement marked a turning point for the status of Korean women. Steeped in patriarchal Confucianism's restriction of women's roles, Korean women were basically "male supporters," working almost entirely behind the scenes. Female status had been reduced to simply being a vehicle for procreation. Christianity, however, revolutionized women's consciousness, awakening them from their deeply internalized sexism and oppression. This is not to say that Korean women throughout history have never made a social impact. Under Buddhism, prior to the emergence of Confucianism, Korea had several female queens. It was Korea's Neo-Confucian social organization that reduced women to second-class status.

Undoubtedly, the gospel message of Jesus Christ touched many

---

3. Wei Jo Kang, *Christ and Caesar in Modern Korea: A History of Christianity and Politics* (Albany: State University of New York, 1997), 51–52.

women's *han* (affliction) and provided them with a channel to recover their dignity as human beings. Through the opportunities of education at the beginning of the twentieth century, women's eyes were opened, and they began to see beyond the bounds of Confucianism. Christianity, therefore, was widely embraced by Korean women from the start as they soaked up its messages of liberation, dignity, and justice. The independence movement became the impetus for women to pour out unyielding resistance against Japanese annexation.

Ironically, the crisis caused by Japanese annexation gave birth to the rise of the social and political leadership of Korean women. It was Japanese colonization that released Korean women from the rules of the patriarchy. Under these unusual circumstances, Korean women went out into the public space to actively participate in their emancipation. During the crisis, no one had the luxury to debate women's roles. Maria Kim and Yu Kwan Soon, among many others, led the resistance movement and transformed women's purpose beyond the traditional privatized position and function. They actively organized and instilled a vision of emancipation in the people during a time of darkness. They became symbols of hope for the Korean people under siege.

Maria Kim, Born to Pioneer Christian Parents

Maria Kim was born on June 18, 1892, in the village of Sorae, and was baptized within a month of her birth. Kim's parents had already been exposed to Christianity by the American Presbyterian missionary Horace G. Underwood. Deeply moved by the gospel, Kim's parents supported Underwood with food, clothing, and living expenses. In addition, her parents released their servants, founded a school, and established the first Korean Christian church, Sorae Presbyterian Church. Firmly committed to women's education, they enrolled Kim in an elementary school run by the Sorae church.[4]

---

4. Suk Ki Chung, *Han Kook Ki Dock Kyo Yeo Sung In Mul Sa* (Korean Christian Women Leaders' History) (Seoul, Korea: Qumran Publisher, 1995), 105–23 (English translation by the author).

When Maria Kim was five years old, her father died from an illness. Her uncle, Yoon Oh Kim, raised her in his house, which was a hub for several pivotal Korean reformers. Determined to further Kim's education, her mother, on her deathbed, put it in her will that Kim was to attend college. Her mother passed away when Kim was thirteen years old.

From an early age, Kim was widely recognized for her extraordinary leadership qualities. She exuded a peaceful presence combined with a sharp consciousness. She was the top student in all her classes. In a society where education existed exclusively for men, girls' mission schools granted women's rights and access to education and thus produced women pioneers like Maria Kim, Yu Kwan Soon, and many others.

From her childhood, Kim had unusual educational opportunities. She continued to study in a girls' mission school in Sorae and also moved to Seoul to attend Jeong Shin, a famous girls' mission school. Upon graduation, she taught at Sophia Women's School and then at Jeong Shin. Through the recommendation of Principal Lewis of Jeong Shin, Kim decided to go to Tokyo in 1914 for further study. At the age of twenty-two, she went to Japan, where Korean students were deeply concerned about the motherland's independence from Japanese rule. At Tokyo Women's College, Kim met an American missionary, Miss London, who mentored her closely and provided her with spiritual guidance.

On January 22, 1919, Korean students in Japan heard the news that King Kojong of Korea had been fatally poisoned by Japanese operatives. Song Gye Back and Pak Kwan Soo then composed the Korean Declaration of Independence. On February 8, 1919, Maria Kim and five hundred Korean students in Tokyo gathered at the Korean YMCA and demonstrated against the Japanese for the murder of Kojong and the annexation. They read the Declaration of Independence and demanded the liberation of Korea. Because of her participation in this demonstration, Kim was arrested by Japanese police and was tortured for eight hours before being released.[5]

---

5. Yeon Oak Yi, *Yeo Jeondohyo Hak* (School of Women's Mission Com-

Upon her release, Maria Kim copied the Declaration of Independence secretly and took on the responsibility of bringing it to Korea despite a tight vigil by the Japanese. Her role in the Korean independence movement is crucial in several ways. She not only led the demonstration in Tokyo that was a precursor to the March First Independence Movement, but she was also instrumental in transporting the secret documents that fueled the March First Movement.

The March First Movement of 1919 took place in 212 cities for sixty consecutive days. Over 1.1 million people participated in 1,214 demonstrations. According to the Presbyterian General Assembly in October 1919, it was reported that Korean male Presbyterian prisoners numbered 2,125, while female prisoners numbered 531.[6]

On March 5, 1919, four days after the March First Independence Movement, Japanese soldiers captured Maria Kim at gunpoint at Jeong Shin, where she taught. As in all cases of colonization, Japanese policy utilized Korean traitors who aligned themselves with the Japanese power structure. It was a Korean traitor who tortured Kim during her inquisition in the prison basement. As she was dragged down the stairs, the screams of many Korean prisoners filled the eerie torture chambers. The following dialogue describes the actual prosecution of Kim by the soldier:

Soldier: "Are you Maria Kim?"

Maria: "Yes."

Soldier: "You must know why you are here?"

Maria: "I don't know why you capture innocent people and torture them."

Soldier: "Is that so? I will explain it. You ignored the emperor's decree and committed an anti-empire crime. Isn't that a crime?"

Maria: "The emperor is your emperor, not Korean. Why is it a crime to recover the sovereignty of my country? You'd better admit

mittee) (Seoul, Korea: Korean Presbyterian Women's Association, 1993), 106–18.

6. Ibid., 112.

that you are the one who is committing a crime by taking over my country by force."[7]

Kim withstood the brutality and torture with courage and bravery. Before she even finished her indictment of Japanese rule, the soldiers assaulted her, whipping her with a leather rod while the Korean traitor assaulted her with kicks to the body. This cruelty almost took her life, but despite being subjected to torture that left her entire body scarred, Kim did not yield. After five months of torture in prison, Kim was finally released on August 4, 1919. She was twenty-six years old.

The flame for liberation from Japan's atrocity was burning even stronger within her following her release. During the celebration of her release, Kim was able to unite various groups of women who had been working toward Korean liberation and was elected president of the Patriotic Women's Group in Korea. The previous version of the group had focused on raising funds for the male leaders of the independence movement. Under Kim's leadership, the Patriotic Women's Group moved into a new phase. The following quote from Kim's inauguration reflects the transition of the organization:

> An old saying urges us to love your country as your household. Even a foolish husband and wife understand that as a family member if we don't love our family, that household cannot be well, as a people if we do not love our country, the country cannot be preserved. Ah! We wives are also part of the people. Toward recovering the national and human rights we must only move forward with no retreat. I urge you to be courageous women and unite for this noble cause.[8]

Her inaugural address stressed the mission of the Patriotic Women's Group as the "recovery of the country" and "recovery of human rights." Under her strong leadership, membership grew quickly. The group was able to accomplish miraculous achievements such as sending six thousand won (Korean currency) to a Korean gov-

---

7. Suk Ki Chung, *Han Kook Ki Dock*, 116–17.
8. Ibid., 119.

ernment in exile in Hawaii. In November of 1919, however, one of the members betrayed the group and reported the movement to a Japanese official. Immediately, more than one thousand women were arrested. By then, Kim's health was severely impaired due to the aftereffects of her earlier imprisonment and torture. Yet her spirituality sustained her with a relentless spirit of courage and perseverance, and she led impassioned prayer meetings in her prison cell. The crueler the torture, the calmer Kim became, even as they fastened a running water hose onto her nose.

Although Kim was sentenced to five years in prison, endless advocacy by missionaries and friends earned her an early release from the hellish torture of her prison cell; but she was now in exile. On July 10, 1921, missionary George S. McCune helped Kim take refuge in Shanghai. During this time of physical recovery, she joined the national independence movement through the Korean government in exile in Shanghai.

While more Korean Christian women were relegated to roles such as Bible sales and door-to-door evangelism, Maria Kim had the rare opportunity to further her ministry and education. In 1923, she came to America. A year later, she enrolled at Park University (in Missouri), where she studied sociology for two years. In 1928, she studied at the University of Chicago and earned a Master of Arts in sociology. In the 1930s, she studied theology at the Biblical Theological Seminary in New York. While in New York, she organized another Patriotic Women's Group and continued her independence movement work. Her constant learning and organizing kept her going in exile.

In 1933, after thirteen years of life in exile, Kim returned to Korea, which was still under Japanese occupation. She taught at Martha Wilson Bible College, where her class on the prophet Jeremiah was flooded with tears from her students. The weeping prophet's message addressed the condition of Korea under siege.[9]

Because of Kim's strong opposition to Shinto worship, the Japanese shut down the school. Kim never recovered from the shock.

---

9. Ibid., 121–22.

She died on March 13, 1944, just one year prior to Korean independence. She was only fifty-three.[10] In Kim's life, we can see faith in action and theological education embodied. Her calm endurance before the cruelty of torture exemplifies courage, spirituality, and authentic power. Her unyielding stance for truth and resistance against evil made the forces of evil timid and powerless. In fact, the oppressor could not shake the depth of Kim's spiritual well within. The theological dispute during postindependence, which split the Korean Presbyterian churches into many pieces, cannot be found in Maria Kim's life. Her life speaks of the wholeness of the gospel, with unyielding spirituality.

Yu Kwan Soon, Korea's Joan of Arc

Another woman resistor was a young Methodist girl named Yu Kwan Soon, who is often referred to as Korea's Joan of Arc. Accounts of her heroism continue to be passed down to every Korean from early childhood, a life story that bears a striking resemblance to that of the early Christians under the Roman Empire.

Born in 1902, Yu Kwan Soon was educated in a mission school in a manner comparable to Maria Kim's early education. Both women's parents were pioneer Korean Christians who embraced Christianity and Western education as a solution for the Korean national struggle. Similar to Maria Kim's parents, Yu's father, Yu Joong Kwon, started a school and established a church in his village. He sought reformation through education and protection in God's grace, and he instilled in Yu a vision for the liberation of Korea even when she was very young. Under her father's spiritual guidance, Yu's vision and leadership for the emancipation began. Her father urged, "Be diligent in learning and become a leader. Do not forget about the labor of emancipation of the lost country."[11]

---

10. Ibid., 119.

11. Hoon Lee Kang, *Chung Sa Ae Bit Nan Soon Kook Sun Yol Dul* (Korean Martyrs) (Seoul, Korea: Yok Sa Pun Chan Hyo, 1990), 640. In Bok Yeo, *Han Kook Eui In Mul* (Korean Leaders) (Seoul, Korea: Yeo Moon Sa, 1972), 182.

Soon after, a female Methodist missionary in the village visited Yu's parents and requested permission to send Yu to Seoul to study at the Methodist Ewha Girls' School. Her parents gladly approved. At the age of thirteen, Yu followed the missionary to Seoul, leaving her parents and friends behind. During her school years, Yu was inspired by the biographies of Joan of Arc and Florence Nightingale.[12] Strongly identifying with these two women, Yu sought to emulate them both in her own way. She ardently envisioned the liberation of the motherland like Joan of Arc and also cultivated the compassionate heart of Florence Nightingale. She embodied both women in her resistance against Japanese annexation. The horizons of time and space were bridged as Yu Kwan Soon identified her life with the inspirational life stories of these two women, sharpening her calling and sense of destiny.

In 1919, three years into her study in Seoul, the March First Independence Movement began. Yu could literally hear the thunder of liberation from the crowds outside her dorm. When she heard that her village was not a part of this independence movement, Yu headed down to her village to organize people. Although she was initially met with resistance because of her youth and the fact that local police were watching carefully, she eventually won the support of the local people. With the help of local church-group elders, she planned and organized a mass demonstration similar to the one in Seoul, this one scheduled for March 1 by the lunar calendar, which happened to fall on April 1. The following is her prayer:

> O, O God, now time has come nearer. May you grant us freedom by removing the enemy, the Japanese. Tomorrow, grant your courage and strength onto the key representatives so that this land may become a happy land of our people. Lord, may you grant courage and strength unto this girl as well. Viva Korean independence! Viva Korean independence![13]

12. Hyo Sop Chung, *Yu Kwan Soon, the Korean Joan of Arc* (Seoul, Korea: Yeo Sung Dong Ah, 1971), 67.

13. *Kook Ga Bo Hoon Cheo, Purun San, Got Eun Sol* (Green Mountain and Straight Pine) (Seoul, Korea: In Ruk Jeong Bo Center [Human Resource Information Center], 1995), 158. (English translation is by the author.)

Yu demonstrated unusual leadership qualities for her age. Traveling from village to village, she informed people of a forthcoming demonstration, asking for representatives to participate in planning meetings. They devised a signal to announce the start of the demonstration—a torch relayed from the mountaintop. The night before the scheduled demonstration, Yu personally climbed the mountain and ignited the torch to signal the gathering the following day at the Aunae Market. Yu addressed the crowd, read the declaration, and led a march through town. The Japanese responded with brutal force, killing nineteen people, including Yu's parents. She and many others were arrested.

Hope beyond Torture

As in the case of Maria Kim, the flame of the independence movement burned even stronger in Yu Kwan Soon while she was imprisoned:

> Yu was first sent to Ch'onan prison where she was tortured for many days before being transferred to Konju prison. She was tried and sentenced to three years in prison. Prison life was extremely harsh; her last words spoken were, "Japan will fall." The Japanese guards then reportedly tore her limbs from her body into many pieces. She died in Sodaemun Prison in Seoul on October 12, 1920. She was sixteen years old.[14]

From her prison cell, Yu had organized a special March First Independence Movement anniversary, and all the prisoners cried out in unison, *"Dae Han Dok Lip Man Se,"* which in English means "Victory for Korea."

Richard Saccone writes:

> This extraordinary young woman with an indefatigable spirit accomplished much, in her short life, to inspire the Korean

---

14. Richard Saccone, *Koreans to Remember: 50 Famous People Who Helped Shape Korea* (Elizabeth, NJ: Hollym International Corp., 1993), 233.

people. Her actions gained the admiration of everyday people and helped them to persevere when they needed hope most.

Saccone also called Yu the "Joan of Arc of Korea" and praised Yu's "ability to organize and incite people to action during the March First Independence Movement in 1919."[15] Yu brought hope in a crisis situation. Mary C. Grey describes this process of generating hope in a hopeless situation in her book *The Outrageous Pursuit of Hope*. Grey quotes the Ghanaian woman theologian Mercy Amba Oduyoye, "Wear hope like a skin." Grey herself stresses, "The more desperate a situation is, the stronger the hope." This kind of hope stretches the limits of what is possible.[16]

Grey describes resistance as follows:

> Resistance is a far deeper concept than simply activism. Because, in the depth of our hearts, we have said "no" to injustice and oppression on a global level, something has been liberated deep within us and in the solidarity of the groups with whom we are in relation. We can recover our collective soul. Resistance springs from the centrality of compassion. This compassion is more than a feeling or emotion. It is rooted in the mothering, womb-like compassion of God.[17]

Demonstrating hope beyond hope, Yu Kwan Soon became a human torch. Yet, researching the documents about her life can be a very frustrating experience. "Her tomb is not well taken care of," laments Rev. Jae Hoon Park, a Korean church music pioneer who composed an opera about Yu Kwan Soon and directed its premiere opening in Seoul, Korea, in March 2000.[18]

---

15. Ibid., 230.

16. Mary C. Grey, *The Outrageous Pursuit of Hope* (New York: Crossroad, 2000), 6.

17. Ibid., 35.

18. I visited Rev. Jae Hoon Park in Toronto. He has retired from his ministry with the Divine Light Presbyterian Church. A conversation with him affirmed frustration with the Korean government and the Methodist denomination because of their neglect of Yu Kwan Soon's memorial site.

Paulo Freire describes the oppressed's struggle for liberation:

> In order for the oppressed to be able to wage the struggle for
> their liberation, they must perceive the reality of oppression
> not as a closed world from which there is no exit, but as a lim-
> iting situation that they can transform. This perception is a
> necessary but not a sufficient condition for liberation; it must
> become the motivating force for liberating action.[19]

The deep resonance with the biblical narrative of struggle for
liberation equipped Yu with hope in the face of unbearable violence, torture, and imprisonment. Prayer without ceasing, morning
and night, and social organization and resistance against evil eventually emancipated the Korean people. Her courage and extraordinary leadership transcended all of the Confucian taboos concerning
gender and age. Remember, her parents died during the initially
peaceful independence gathering when the Japanese killed people
to disperse the crowds. Imagine the pain of losing her parents,
leaving her younger siblings as orphans, and undergoing imprisonment and death. Demonstrating hope beyond hope, Yu Kwan Soon
became a light in the dark, signaling the call to resistance.

Resistance Leadership

From the lives of Maria Kim and Yu Kwan Soon, we can draw
out key principles for forming resistance leadership. Completely
unarmed, these women resistors maintained a spirit of "if I perish, I perish" that threatened the fully armed colonizer. Guns could
not defeat their relentless courage and faith in God. Their fearless
leadership emerged from the combination of divine providence,
extraordinary parental support, Christian education, a uniquely
historical moment, and their faith in God.

Both Maria Kim and Yu Kwan Soon were raised by devout first-
generation Korean Christian parents. Both women's parents recognized extraordinary leadership qualities in their daughters. Both

---

19. Paulo Freire, *The Pedagogy of the Oppressed* (New York: Seabury
Press, 1970), 34.

women had access to education through mission schools established by Presbyterian and Methodist missionaries. The holistic spirituality of both Kim and Yu reveals one of the most important contributions of Western mission's dedication to women's education at a time when Korean society offered educational opportunities only for men. From these early formative experiences, Kim and Yu dedicated their lives to the emancipation of the motherland. Both were women of fervent prayer and action. Inspired by the gospel of justice, liberation, and human dignity, they demonstrated great leadership and courage in dire circumstances, and they brought life to the Korean people in darkness. They were able to inspire and mobilize people to resist injustice. Just as Stephen was stoned to death as truth prevailed and the good news spread, these courageous women died for the cause of resisting injustice. The gospel took on political forces, and in the social context of Korea, it imbued hope for liberation.

Their life-giving example through life-relinquishing sacrifice provides a model for liberating the schismatic trap of Korean Christianity. In the Christian witness of Kim and Yu, we do not find the division between proclamation and social action that plagues post-independence Korean Christianity. The leadership example of these women is once again needed as Korea faces a less visible and far subtler crisis in the form of the cultural-economic force of coca-colonization. The names Maria Kim and Yu Kwan Soon embody the Christian characteristics of courage, strength, and redemption for a crisis-ridden country. Paradoxically, under crisis, early stage Korean Christianity showed the greatest maturity. Korean Christianity exemplified integrity with courageous leadership at its origin.

As the word "crisis" in Chinese characters connotes both danger and opportunity, during one of the darkest moments in Korean history, Kim and Yu took action, demonstrating courage and strength. Their zeal and courage inspired the nation and provided a unified spirit toward independence, but the precious spirit and action of these two Korean women have been buried. How regrettable it is that today's Korean Christians do not remember their stories. How absurd it is to see churches entrenched by the old sacred cows of conservatism versus liberalism, splitting the gospel into many pieces. How disheartening to see the churches lacking vision, mission, and a sense of history and justice. Korean Christianity, which once bore such powerful Christian witness, stands by timidly as the Korean version of Constantinization diminishes the integrity of the church. The stories of these two patriotic women and their unyielding spirit of "if I perish, I perish" need to be transmitted to succeeding generations.

Yinish Surrender and Yangish Resistance

The lives of Maria Kim and Yu Kwan Soon exude the paradoxical duality of yin and yang, expressed through two dynamics. The first is a dialectical duality of pacifistic inner surrender to death (yin) and subversive outer social resistance (yang). Out of such inner tranquility flows the yangish subversive resistance of the two women. The outer resistance (yang) without being grounded in the inner surrender (yin) could not endure brutal oppression. The second is the dualistic intergroup dynamic of yin (the oppressed) and yang (the oppressor). The oppressed here are Kim and Yu, who have consciousness (yin), and the oppressor, the Japanese colonizers (yang), who lack consciousness. The oppressor, lacking power flowing from within (yin), asserts power by domination (yang). The redemption of such oppressors can begin only when they are willing to journey within and discover the oppressed within (yin). From the false dichotomy of yang versus yin, the oppressor needs to shift toward a duality of yin and yang, as demonstrated by these two Korean women resistors.

Without freedom from fear of death, such fearless resistance against the overwhelmingly armed Japanese soldiers cannot be imagined. Our own Lord Jesus Christ embodied the authentic courage emerging from total surrender to death. The Gospel of John contains the paradoxical duality of both yin and yang as Jesus deals with earthly authority through godly authority. Jesus says,

> For this reason the Father loves me, because I lay down my life in order to take it up again. No one takes it from me, but I lay it down of my own accord. I have power to lay it down, and I

have power to take it up again. I have received this command
from my Father. (John 10:17–18)

Jesus, an innocent man, carrying the cross of criminals, subverts
perverted power. The cross was an instrument for violent punishment, but Jesus redeemed it for the purpose of life-giving replenishment. Because he was so centered on God's will within, Jesus was
able to oppose the Roman culture of punishment with a redemptive
replenishment. The yinish subversion of yangish perversion of Jewish and Roman power is embodied in Jesus's crucifixion.

There is a purifying power in subversive resistance against evil
forces. The external force, although able to break the human body,
cannot break the internal human spirit as long as one is willing to
drink from the bitter cup of death. Death no longer has power over
those who let go of life. In the dialectic duality of yin and yang,
death no longer is the opposite of life. They are paradoxically one.
Jesus's total obedience to death exemplifies the subversive power
of the cross. He invited his disciples to take up the cross as well, as
they were commissioned to continue his ministry.

"If you lose your life, you will gain your life" (Luke 9:24)
expresses the essence of Kim and Yu, two extraordinary Korean
Christian pioneer women. Their readiness to die for the cause of
liberation did not allow any room for fear. This is a precious lesson
in how to find freedom from bondage. The power of domination
and control persists only as long as people, in fear of death, conform to rather than resist evil. Freedom from fear of death leads to
courage; courage leads to action.

From *Daejung* to *Minjung*

There is an inside-out spirituality that can transform "the masses"
into "the people." Jin-Kwan Kwon differentiates "the masses"
(*daejung*) from "the people" (*minjung*). He defines "the people" as:

Those whose social consciousness is critical, and consequently, those whose readiness to undertake new historical
tasks is intense. The term "the people" emphasizes the state
of a people who are self-conscious and critical of their own
political situation by differentiating themselves from the situ-

ation. The masses are not conscious of their own situation. They live *within* the situation where they happen to find themselves. The masses are not self-conscious of their collective interests and do not act upon the structure that binds them in bondage.[20]

Both Kim and Yu conscientized the masses, bringing awareness to them and transforming *daejung* into *minjung*. Their ability to transform the masses into the people with a collective consciousness stems from the deep spirituality of prayer.

Despite such solid examples of holistic faith in its history, Korean Christianity has pushed aside these historical movements and thus stands on the verge of spiritual starvation. Conforming to the status quo, Korean churches are busy reaching the masses but not the people. Thus, they continue to fail in their prophetic role. A large number of Korean Christians remain silent as objects of the status quo with their eyes and ears closed to the crucial historical developments of today.

Korean Christianity started among the *minjung* and for the *minjung*, identifying with the *minjung*'s struggle. Where has the spirit of courage and truth gone? Do the martyrs who have shed their blood deserve the heritage of such division in the nation? The external crisis has turned inward, with people torturing one another as if the colonizer's chain still binds. Where are Korean women's passions today? With what are they consumed? Do we need another crisis in order to recover our lost consciousness?

Anesthetization of Consciousness during Postindependence

Unlike the overtly violent military colonization perpetrated by imperial Japan, the current coca-colonization of Korea works on an insidious level, numbing human consciousness and leaving it

---

20. Jin-Kwan Kwon, "Minjung Theology and Its Future Task for People's Movement: A Theological Refection on the Theme of Religion, Power and Politics in the Korean Context," *CTC Bulletin* 10 (May-December, 1991): 17.

vulnerable as economic prey. As the Constantinization of Christianity desensitizes the spirit of resistance under persecution, the resistance of the early Korean Christians against the Japanese was also domesticated with the expansion of the Korean church.

Aloysius Pieris rightly critiques comfortably mammonized Christianity, which "hinders the church for its role as *a messianic* people."[21] Mammonized Korean Christianity resulted from a lack of theologizing during critical moments in Korean church history. Whereas the emphasis of indigenized Christianity in Korea through the Nevius mission policy[22] has its strengths, a negative aspect is the minimizing of pastoral education. The consequence of keeping pastoral leadership at a minimum kept the Korean churches on the back burner when radical paradigmatic global changes began during the 1920s. Unlike the church that was at the forefront of the March First Independence Movement in 1919, the later Korean church lagged behind societal demands while emphasizing an otherworldly revival. It lacked theological backbone even to respond, let alone lead, when faced with complex challenges from within and without. This sadly left Korean Christianity divided into two separate branches during this period: the church-centered, otherworldly revival church and the church of the sociopolitical gospel that sought to continue the spirit of the March First Independence Movement.[23]

The American Presbyterian denomination's mission policy for the Korean Peninsula after Korea's independence set the course for Korean Protestant Christianity. Affected by the emergence of the liberal voice in America, a staunch conservative camp represented mission work in Korea, with its dualistic split of conservative

---

21. Aloysius Pieris, SJ, *Fire and Water: Basic Issues in Asian Buddhism and Christianity* (Maryknoll, NY: Orbis Books, 1996), 72.

22. See John Livingston Nevius, *The Planting and Development of Missionary Churches* (New York: Foreign Mission Library, 1899). The Nevius Plan outlined five points for mission that were designed to be respectful of nature cultures and state power.

23. Institute of Korean Church History Studies, *A History of the Korean Church* (Seoul, Korea: Christian Literature Press, 1989), 301–2.

against liberal and this world against the otherworld. Regrettably, the spirit of the independence movement was quickly renounced rather than honored. Once the external force of oppression was lifted, there was no forum for processing pain and hurt. The painful *han*[24] from thirty-five years of oppression was simply denied. A country in deep need of recovery from external wounds and internal pain turned to an otherworldly theology imposed by the missionary policy, burying the tension and leaving unresolved issues in a state of suspension.

Elevating revivalists, the missionary policy of the Presbyterian Church offered no room for sociopolitical activists who firmly grounded their actions in biblical narratives. Christian thinkers with a deep consciousness could not quench their thirst within the church, and many who could have provided leadership in giving birth to theological identity left the church. Many young and inspirational leaders could not find a niche in the otherworldly churches and thus turned to communism. Therefore, regrettably, the marvelous Christian leadership demonstrated during the crisis was lost.

Consequently, Korean Christianity quickly resorted to the revival track and became fixed on an otherworldly theology and culture, splitting denominations and churches into many pieces. The postindependence Christianity, under the rise of fundamentalism in the American context, shifted a once holistic gospel into a dualistic, otherworldly one. Under the otherworldly mission endeavor, the transmission of the pioneers' consciousness of resistance was obstructed, leaving several lasting implications for Korean Protestant Christianity.

First, anti-intellectualism permeated Korean Christianity and remains today. The result was a split between the spiritually oriented group and the social action–oriented group, bitterly dividing the Korean body of Christ. Second, having lost the golden opportunity to build theological identity, Korean Christianity became dogmatic and busy with hair-splitting doctrinal arguments. Third, before the division of the 38th parallel in 1945, doctrinal and denominational divisions were drawn along the

---

24. A Korean cultural trait meaning sorrow, regret, etc.

38th parallel (the dividing line between North and South Korea). Fourth, Christianity, once an inspiration for a unified movement of independence, was polarized. In the south, it was characterized by otherworldly revivalism, and in the north, by atheistic communism. The divided Korean Peninsula symbolizes a divided Christian theology of the left and the right. Finally, today's Korean Christianity, despite its numerical growth, is greatly hindered in its role in society and in the mission of transformation. It is as if one is expanding a house without checking the beams and structures that support the house.

The result of the divided gospel between the social and spiritual is the deadening of consciousness and an anesthetized Christianity in the face of coca-colonization. Despite powerful examples of a Christianity that transformed *daejung* into *minjung,* the current Christianity exhibits depoliticized and privatized practice. Aloysius Pieris critiques Korean Christianity: "Collusion between the neocolonialist Christianity and developmentalist ideology conspires to keep the unshepherded masses (*daejung*) from leaving their chains and exercising their role as a messianic people (*minjung*)."[25]

The cold war on the Korean Peninsula, more than half a century old, mirrors a deep-seated theological split as well. In a culture of hypermaterialism, the difficulty today lies in the death of consciousness due to the decline of education. The visible, long-standing cease-fire, however, can also paralyze the consciousness of the people and cause them to be vulnerable to materialism in lieu of resistance. The challenge lies in the fact that many people have to come out of their comfort zones and see the urgent need to bring reconciliation between the two divided governments. Those who suffer most, the separated family members, are reaching their last years on earth. This task demands sacrificial leadership such as that demonstrated by Yu Kwan Soon and Maria Kim. Yet the politicization of unification issues has been pervasive among both politicians and Christian leaders.

Meanwhile, Protestant Christianity confines the gospel within the four walls of the church building and thus dichotomizes faith

---

25. Ibid.

and the world. Sadly, the power of the gospel remains relatively invisible in society despite the expansion of Christianity. Meanwhile, Korean society as a whole is seduced by wholesale globalization, leaving its people in desperate need of authentic inner transformation. Once again, numerous prophets in action are needed as the country confronts an unavoidable crisis: national humiliation from the financial corruption that led to national bankruptcy. Christianity without the cross perverts itself into mammonism.

Implications for Theological Education

Although Korean Christianity has reached remarkable numeric growth alongside modernization, theological growth has not accompanied it. Internalization of the gospel and a sense of history continue to diminish. As Korean Christianity plateaus and embarks on a declining phase, this may be the time to examine our Christian history rigorously.

The very structure and content of theological education have to be challenged and transformed. The mass production of theological education in general lacks personal contact. Education in this scenario functions as a delivery system for knowledge in isolation. A true Christian education embodies the nature of discipleship. Both prophetic and institutional leadership must coexist and create a symbiotic organism of constantly evolving and maturing theological education.

From the lives of Kim and Yu, we can see the impact of education, which awakened them to confront their reality and embrace hope beyond hope. Regretfully, such stories are absent in the Westernized theological education curriculum. In turn, Korean seminary students spend more time copying Western theologies, graduating with a theological identity with no roots in the Korean context or history. Korean theological education needs genuine educational reform, developing an indigenous identity instead of regurgitating a photocopy of Western theology.

We can draw universal principles of resistance for the particular contexts of today, just as Maria Kim and Yu Kwan Soon connected with biblical contexts of early Christians under siege. The weeping prophet Jeremiah's stories were their stories. If the stories of Joan of Arc and Florence Nightingale inspired a Korean girl like Yu Kwan Soon, then the stories of Yu and Kim should all the more inspire the current generation in identity crisis. Despite unimaginable obstacles, the authenticity and integrity of humanity demonstrated by these women transcend time and space, collapsing cultural, geographical, and historical horizons. Their life examples intersect our lives today. Such stories shape identity and conscientize *daejung* to become *minjung*. For such conscientization to take place, educators need to be awakened from the effects of materialism and step into the long-awaited indigenizing process.

Amid the titanic impacts of mammonism, consumerism, and expansionism, Korean society once again confronts the challenge of reformation. The severe moral decay in all segments of Korean society calls for the radical processes of internal purification. In reshaping Christian identity, reconnecting with the forgotten stories of women pioneers like Maria Kim and Yu Kwan Soon is crucial.

Lack of Christian identity tarnishes the legacy of these female saints who offered their lives so selflessly. The present situation is like the ground in a dry season, waiting to be soaked. Theological educators today must provide students with a sense of history and identity rooted in Korean history so that they may grasp a vision grounded in an accurate perception of reality.

The challenge of today's resistance movement is to drink from our own theological well and rediscover the holistic duality of yin and yang. By lifting up these courageous legacies of Yu and Kim, the current and forthcoming generation of women may once again carry the spirit of justice and liberation. It is our responsibility to continue what Yu and Kim demonstrated so fiercely and so purely for equality, justice, and salvation for all people.

Channelling Czech statesman and writer Vaclav Havel, Parker Palmer describes the authentic leadership that Korean Christians need:

The power for authentic leadership, Havel tells us, is found not in external arrangements but in the human heart. Authen-

tic leaders in every setting—from families to nation states—
aim at liberating the heart, their own and others', so that its
powers can liberate the world.[26]

An inside-out journey of resistance may flow like "rivers of living
water" (John 7:38). The holistic duality of yin and yang offers a rich
theological lens through which we can theologize and indigenize.
Revisiting Maria Kim and Yu Kwan Soon is a ritual of retelling
stories of self-affirmation and life. Their lives embody resistance
rooted in the womb-like compassion of God, conscientized by the
liberating messages of Jesus Christ, transcending injustice in their
time and hopefully ours as well.

26. Parker Palmer, *Let Your Life Speak: Listening for the Voice of Vocation* (San Francisco: Jossey-Bass Publishers, 2000), 76.

Asian American Women in the Workplace and the Church

The ideal for a community is the mutual acceptance of all persons as valued members. In a nurturing and productive community, persons of diverse character and talent contribute to the welfare of the whole. Diversity is accepted as a reality of life and differences are viewed harmoniously. The yin and yang explanation of life implies the wisdom of such a pattern of living.

However, in many Asian American congregations, the ideal of a community of diverse elements in harmonious relationship is not fully realized. Asian practices have been influenced by thousands of years of interpretation of Confucian and other social systems of relationships. What originally were benevolent principles of mutuality, reciprocity, respect, and good will demonstrated by the practice of rites and proprieties have devolved into codes and regulations directing young people to obey their elders and women to submit to men.

Asian American professional women face special problems regarding roles and relationships. Working outside the home, these women's efforts are resisted or rejected by those who hold power and authority in churches and professional organizations.

David Ng, organizer for Lilly's Project—
People on the Way

Five Levels of Power

The feminist movement does not capture the hearts of Asian American women. With its privileged status and different reality, this movement of white, middle- and upper-class women does not represent the realities Asian American women face in their homes, workplaces, or churches. Amid the tension between cultural and theological worlds, we have no particular movement with which we may identity, and we are thus apt to be theological and cultural orphans.

Given that reality, it is crucial to give voice to the peculiar struggles of Asian American women on the front lines of Christian leadership. Estranged from the feminist movement and blocked by our respective ethnic groups, women of Asian heritage seek our own identity and integrity—our own call to being. We understand this call to Asian American women to be a call from God, a call into the body of Christ.

This chapter focuses on the treatment of Asian professional women both in the workplace and in the church. It analyzes factors that wound and divide the body of Christ. Issues of power and authority are daily struggles for women who are pioneers in a man's world. Power dynamics exist in every relationship because relationships encompass gender, ethnicity, class, and generations. In *Power and Innocence*, Rollo May analyzes the basic human need for power and the impact of its absence on the human being. I will use his five levels of power as a framework for ethnic, gender, class, and generational issues. They are (1) the power to be; (2) self-affirmation; (3) self-assertion; (4) aggression; and (5) violence.

These power dynamics interact and weave together the tapestry of one's life cycle. May offers wise counsel: a healthy community pays attention to both individual and collective attitudes toward power dynamics.[1]

---

1. Rollo May, *Power and Innocence: A Search for the Sources of Violence* (New York: W.W. Norton, 1972), 40–45.

The Power to Be

The expression "the power to be" is the demand for basic survival, as shown when a newborn baby cries or reaches out its arms. Not to express this basic need for survival is considered abnormal. The power to be is an essential element in the development of personality. May stresses that when this power to be is denied, "neurosis, psychosis, or violence will result."[2]

The minority professional woman's triple marginality—being a woman instead of a man, being the minority instead of the majority, and being marginalized among women—induces alienation and pain. The philosopher Søren Kierkegaard empathized with the affliction of women when he said that "the misfortune of women is that at a given moment they are all important, while the next day they are completely unimportant."[3] And when women perceive that men control power, this leads them to seek affirmation from males rather than females.

Hyun Sung,[4] a Korean American in her first year in the workplace of a Christian organization, suffered as a woman in a man's world:

> In my loneliness at the workplace, I sought some friendships with mainstream women. In this competitive environment, I found it difficult to move beyond superficial cliché relationships. Especially when my work was productive, they ignored me. Jane, a white woman with an influential position in the finance department, has been with this organization for more than ten years. Jane gives all her time and energy to the powerful male leaders while ignoring me. She shields her time from women with potential by not returning their phone calls

---

2. Ibid.

3. Gustavo Gutiérrez, *The God of Life* (Maryknoll, NY: Orbis Books, 1989), 166.

4. All names have been changed in the personal narratives in this chapter. These stories emerged from both my ecclesial ministry from 1990 to 1995 and from my time as a member of the faculty at Fuller Theological Seminary from 1993 to 1998.

or by canceling appointments at the last minute. Jane herself is very reactionary when she experiences this same treatment from the male leaders.

Why do women like Jane who already have enough clout continue to seek solidarity with powerful males? It appears that self-interest overrides a desire to empower those of like gender. When women seek affirmation from men, it can be understood as a strong desire of the powerless to identify with the powerful. This negates the power of being woman. Women thus spurn one another, treating colleagues as objects of competition.

Gordon Allport warns that a minority person's hostility and denial of his or her minority culture may produce internalized "racial self-hatred." He illustrates the observation of Jews in Nazi concentration camps:

> Studies of Nazi concentration camps show that identification with one's oppressor was a form of adjustment. . . . At first, prisoners tried to keep their self respect intact, to feel inward contempt for their persecutors, to try by stealth and cunning to preserve their lives and their health. But after two or three years of extreme suffering, many of them found that their efforts to please their guards led to a mental surrender. They imitated the guards, wore bits of their clothing (symbolic power), turned against new prisoners, became anti-Semites, and in general took over the dark mentality of the oppressor.[5]

Allport points to two consequences of self-hatred: violence and a derogatory attitude toward one's own group. The strong attempt to identify with the symbolic America depicted by the mass media contributes to the crisis among minority groups. Asian American young people internalize white American physical images as symbolic power. Thus, minority people do not give value to another minority professional unless that person is widely recognized. When Asian professional women meet new people, they find them-

---

5. Gordon Allport, *The Nature of Prejudice* (Cambridge, MA: Addison-Wesley, 1955).

selves in an ambiguous category that makes them feel like non-beings.

The Denial of a Female's Being

Wendy is an ordained minister in her thirties who looks younger than her age. She shares her struggle in trying to do ministry in a congregational setting:

> People who do not know me treat me as a secretary and tell me to make copies for them. Once they find out that I am a pastor, they often cannot hide their surprise and do not know what to do with me. Unless I become a nationally known figure, this experience will continue. The flip side of this is in the case of the male. A friend of mine is not a pastor. Yet, with his tall height and gentle appearance, people call him a pastor. Ironically, he has to correct people that he is not a pastor.

How can a female minister overcome her social disposition in a world of power images? Since both Eastern and Western images of authority are external and shaped by the dominant groups, men and women need to work together harmoniously to bring changes in perception in order for Asian American female leadership to be accepted. When society does not provide suitable images for their positions, women like Hyun Sung and Wendy undergo endless embarrassing encounters with people in both the minority and dominant cultures, who fail to recognize their legitimate power to be. Consequently, women on the front lines are haunted with a stronger sense of homelessness in an already homeless postmodern world. We need tremendous inner strength in order to continue our struggle against nonbeing as we journey toward a sense of dignity.

Self-Affirmation

We all have the basic need to be affirmed for who we are as well as who we are becoming. Our self-consciousness is shaped by the affirmation of others. This is why the cry for recognition becomes our cry as Asian American women.[6]

---

6. May, *Power and Innocence*, 41.

Ambiguity as a Mechanism of Degradation

Esther, who holds a PhD in theology, teaches at an Asian American seminary. She expresses her treatment as a "nonbeing" by an administrator at that seminary:

> I am popular among the students because I add a fresh teaching style. One year when I asked for the class schedule, an administrator replied evasively, "We have not decided our schedule yet." I said that I would like to teach during the spring quarter. When I called back two weeks later, the man said that the schedule had been completed and that I was not scheduled to teach in the spring. I told him that I had been counting on teaching in the spring and had arranged my other schedule around it. The man simply gave the phone to his coworker and delegated his response. The man under him took the blame and apologized.

Why did the administrator, also an ordained pastor, avoid answering Esther? He felt no obligation or accountability to a woman, no matter what her position. Female status was thus overruled by power and position. Gender hierarchy compelled by the face-saving mechanism of Asian culture heightens the degradation experienced by women. When a verbal agreement is not kept, it is easily covered up by a verbal apology, which avoids an honest and responsible answer. Being treated with ambiguity is more painful than a direct assault because it treats a person as a nonbeing. The administrator did not view Esther as important enough for him to feel the need to explain his mistake.

Verbal agreements rather than written contracts give no protection for someone like Esther. This cultural form of communication relies heavily on the relational dimension in decision making rather than on factual information. Esther often thinks of how an Asian man in her position would be treated. She feels she has been treated like a ghost.

Conditional love—based on certain conditions being met—is self-diminishing rather than self-affirming. The woman who is forced to respond to conditional love sets out on a course of destructive competitiveness. Her self-affirmation is taken by others to be a diminishing of them, and then she in turn is diminished by them.[7]

When self-affirmation meets resistance, we move on to the next level, self-assertion. But many women find it difficult to assert themselves because of patriarchal, cultural, and theological obstacles. Instead, some women find it easier to use manipulation to gain power rather than to assert themselves directly. For Asian females, triple marginality afflicts our humanity. On the one hand, in our attempts to earn legitimacy in professional work, we face ambiguity from the dominant white society—we get token treatment. On the other hand, in decision-making processes, we also suffer ambiguity, resulting in exclusion, as in Esther's case.

Gender as a Tool

In the workplace, women observe how other women behave in interpersonal relationships with the opposite sex. Wendy observes how her coworker Sally, a Christian education director, interacts with men differently than with women. Wendy shares her experience:

> When I try to talk with Sally, she normally keeps it brief. When she talks with male coworkers, I notice that her tone of voice changes. Her countenance is open and accepting. She usually gives eye contact to males as if to draw their attention to herself. Her body gesture is inviting and far more personal. This contrast makes the working relationship with her difficult.

Sally is thus using her gender as a tool to strengthen her relationships with her male coworkers, while limiting her interactions with her female coworker, Wendy. Understandably, Wendy finds this problematic.

Sexual Charm

Why are feminine qualities reduced to sexual charm? What is the impact on society when more females are employed in the public

---

7. Ibid.

sector? Our fast-paced society drives people to take shortcuts in every aspect of life. Climbing up the career ladder is no exception. The flip side of the oppression of women because of gender and race is the manipulation of feminine characteristics. Sexual charm becomes a handy way of dealing with the male-dominant hierarchy. Some women maximize this biological trait to achieve whatever goals they have. When women choose this route, they alienate other women or fall into competition with one another. Then, every woman loses.

We need to guard against this seemingly easy access to power at the expense of degrading who we are. If society rewards those who focus on integrity and morality, our humanity need not be sacrificed by the powerful force of compromise.

Sexual Harassment

The reversal of the use of sexual charm is sexual harassment of women by the male power holders. In the workplace, many women find themselves daily in vulnerable situations. The fine line in drawing the proper physical boundary varies, thus confusing both males and females. Knowing their jobs are at stake, many women find it extremely difficult to confront uncomfortable physical treatment from their male bosses. While white females have a clear definition of sexual harassment, the Asian community has only blurry boundaries.

In an Asian American congregation, Julie, a Christian education director felt a prominent church lay leader pat her on the rear. At first, she did not know what was going on. He repeated his behavior several times in spite of her verbal disapproval. Then Julie started observing him patting other women in the church. When she finally shamed him in front of the people by calling attention to his action as he did it, he finally stopped touching her. Julie was fully aware of the consequences. Ever since her confrontation in front of others, when Julie has tried to get the session's approval for church matters, he has blocked it.

Must women like Julie repress their own sexuality in order to function as leaders in Asian American churches? Not in Julie's case.

She refused to sacrifice her power to be for the sake of ministry. She refused to degrade herself in order to serve the church. Janet Hagberg rightly advocates that the powerless seek action against dehumanizing experiences. She says, "Women, minorities, and certainly the poor . . . may feel more of the chronic powerlessness that can over time be demoralizing unless they take some action on their own behalf."[8]

Self-Assertion

Self-assertion is more overt than self-affirmation and is therefore a stronger form of behavior. The ability to assert oneself is generally a healthy trait, particularly for women.

Assertiveness versus Aggressiveness

Often a female's assertiveness is labeled as aggressiveness by males defining feminine qualities. After all, female assertiveness contradicts the traditional evangelical perception of women as submissive. This theological oppression of women's humanity is far more difficult to change than cultural oppression. Out in the world, women's lifestyles have been liberated because of rapid cultural change. However, the constant use of male-centered interpretation of biblical passages in the church serves to harass many women. Thus, a large number of Christian women suffer a more severe internal conflict than non-Christian women. The following story of Meigan expresses this pain:

> "But you're a woman." As a staff person in a parachurch college campus fellowship group, I often have been affirmed through a recognition of my gifts for ministry. But sometimes, the response is that "this is great, but you're a woman." When I teach effectively or make a significant contribution, credit is given that I as a person can do well; but when I do not speak or teach well, it is often blamed on the fact that I am a woman.

---

8. Janet Hagberg, *Real Power: Stages of Personal Power in Organizations* (Minneapolis: Winston Press, 1994), xxiii.

Must a woman compartmentalize her being and her gender? Gender discrimination is hard to bear because it is an ascribed status, not an achieved status. We did not choose our gender; therefore, we do not bear responsibility for being female. Rather than achieving legitimate authority through our ministry, Asian American women are evaluated according to how well we serve the image of the submissive woman. This is the injustice of gender inequality.

Letting the Men Look Good

June Myung, a 1.5 generation Korean American, is very bright and has natural leadership qualities. She shares the internal dissonance in her leadership role at church:

> I am so burnt out and frustrated with this special interchurch young adult conference. In the middle of the conference preparations, the president of the young adult group moved away. As the vice president, I had to proceed in leadership alone. I received a cold-shoulder response from the group, especially from the guys. They were laid-back, passive, and apathetic because they did not want a woman to be active. I was in tears. They said that they felt burdened when they saw me. They feared that I would give them a job or ask them for help. One guy told me that people who grew up in the United States do not like to be told what to do. They get rebellious even if they were going to do it anyway. He added, "Men do not like to be told by a woman what to do." When I asked him about the work to be done, he replied, "Just leave it. Don't worry about the work."

How can people make sense of conflicting subcultural norms in the early stages of immigrant life? Does "making men look good" take precedence over a woman serving God? As Asian American women acculturate, the strongly held value of women's submissiveness is threatened. Ironically, the rate of Asian women's acculturation into American society is quicker than men's because, at least externally, American society affirms gender equality.

June's conflict in serving the church is indicative of the widening gap of gender inequality for Christian women in the immigrant church. Our acculturation into American culture and our active service in the church challenge the male-dominant structure. Even when the young adult males in June Myung's case had no desire to assume leadership themselves, they blocked a woman's willingness to take the leadership role. In this particular group, a "let the boat sink" mentality prevailed.

Blaming the Victim

Anne recounts the difficulties she faced after finishing her MBA and starting her first job with a Christian business corporation:

> I seem to be a token Asian woman in this Anglo-Christian corporation, hired in order to portray multicultural standards. Since this is my first job in an American business corporation, I do not understand the terms by which the corporation evaluated me. After six months, I still had not gone through an evaluation. Due to financial troubles, workers are overworked and receive low pay. Consequently, the competition for survival is severe and individualism is reinforced. This has left me totally confused. Toward the end of the first year, I started feeling bitter because the executives were measuring me against experienced senior workers. I was criticized because I did not meet the quotas according to experienced standards. When asserting my needs for getting the same opportunities as senior workers against whom I was measured, I ended up being labeled as "pushy."

How can the powerless express their experience without being judged by the power holder's norms? Anne experiences another form of hierarchy called corporate classism. As the only minority woman, her presence itself creates discomfort in the dominant group. When Anne tries to voice her reality, of which the dominant group has no clue, she is viewed as being out of line. Anne, knowing her basic need to be is not being met, starts asserting herself, only to be perceived by the corporation as aggressive.

Liberation theologian Leonardo Boff accurately observes that life at the margins screams at you.[9] The condition that causes screaming is rarely noticed by the people at the center, who only hear the screaming once in a while and feel uncomfortable. The question of who is causing the screaming is rarely addressed. With corporate culture ignorant of the working conditions of the people outside the inner circle, life in the corporation continues, and the wheels of injustice grind on.

Sociologist William Ryan states that "the generic process of blaming the victim is applied to almost every American problem" of inequality—class, race, and gender.[10] However, this is not limited to American society. It is a universal phenomenon, with roots that can be traced back to Genesis: the fallen nature of human beings. But people do not make the theological connection. Expressions of our triple marginality and oppression fall on deaf ears, and our behavior is labeled aggressive. We are employed because of our gender and ethnicity, not only because of our qualifications. When we are employed by the dominant institutions as mere tokens on the bases of our gender and ethnicity, we feel all the more marginalized.

The categories of the dominant group by which we are assessed exclude us. We feel a triple injustice is being done to us because of the already-biased categories of gender and ethnicity. The first injustice is the fact that Asian professional women experience criticism for going against the traditional gender hierarchy in our own community. Second, we therefore feel a severe internal conflict concerning who we are. Third, we experience a different form of exclusion from the dominant culture, a tokenism based on our gender and ethnicity.

Confronted with these triple exclusions, some Asian professional women cry out and are blamed for complaining by the power holders as well as by their own ethnic group. The root cause of our cry is not considered, and the symptom, crying, is condemned.

---

9. Leonardo Boff, *Faith on the Edge* (San Francisco: Harper & Row, 1989), 40.

10. William Ryan, *Blaming the Victim*, revised and updated (New York: Vintage Books, 1976), 5.

Unfortunately, this triple marginal experience affirms the "blaming the victim" theory. When an Asian woman is a token in the dominant institution, there is no category for her, so she is labeled with the categories of the dominant culture. This stereotyping is a form of victimization.

Anne, in her thirties, faces a double patriarchy: from her own ethnic group and from the dominant group. Her own ethnic people do not want to identify with her when they can identify with the prestigious dominant professionals. The flip side of this is that the minority group accepts the dominant group's deviation from traditional values while rejecting the females within its own group. The dominant power holders deny even the slightest hint of sexism and racism. The power elite rejects the idea that these are gender and ethnicity issues and makes personality the focus. Thus, the powerful place blame on the powerless. The heightened awareness of sexism and racism by the powerful is covered up. Frequently, this "blaming the victim" power structure leaves the burden of empowerment up to the powerless. The victim has to find her own relief.

Alienation through "In-Betweenness"

Multiracial Asian American women Naomi Southard and Rita Nakashima Brock affirm the lonely marginal reality of Asian American women in ministry:

> The personal experience of being marginalized and alienated from Western and Eastern cultures is magnified in our professional struggles. An Asian American woman in ministry has crossed significant barriers of culture and tradition in order to fulfill her calling.[11]

The Asian American professional woman's energy is diluted because there is no dependable foundation on which to stand. The lack of power to be and the inability to fit into the image of either the minority or the dominant cultural group strip the woman of

---

11. Naomi Southard and Rita Nakashima Brock, "The Other Half of the Basket: Asian American Women and the Search for a Theological Home," *Journal of Feminist Studies in Religion* 3, no. 2 (Fall 1987): 138.

authority and legitimacy. Such women are driven to constantly excel in their job performance, which leads to accusations that they are not acting appropriately "for a woman," or for a woman of their ethnicity. In other words, it requires a superwoman to survive in the professional world as a minority female while being criticized for being a superwoman!

As May observes, in the Arthur Miller play *Death of a Salesman*, the outcry of Willy Loman's wife calls us to treat fellow humans as human:

> Attention must be paid. . . . Even though "Willy Loman never made a lot of money. His name was never in papers . . . he's a human being. . . . So attention must be paid."[12]

Like Willy Loman's wife, minority people sometimes personalize another minority's unjust experience and assert it for themselves. May describes this as an indirect assertion of ourselves.

Aggression

Following May's understanding, aggression is a built-in emotional reaction that results from the violation of one's self-assertion. A psychological cause of aggression is the denial of a healthy response to one's assertion. The following story about Keiko describes how female assertiveness is perceived as aggressiveness by most Asian females, a perception that stems from both cultural and theological patriarchy:

> There was a forum on Asian American Ministry at a local church. The panelists were Asian American males. When the subject turned to the issue of female leadership, a male professional expressed typical Christian jargon. "Women should be silent in the church. This applies today because biblical truth does not change with time." At this, an Asian American female professional disagreed. The male erupted at the female's disagreement.

---

12. May, *Power and Innocence*, 41.

Should women be silent in the church at all times? Why were women allowed to prophesy in the New Testament (Acts 21:9; 1 Corinthians 11:5; Luke 1:46)? Can theology and hermeneutics be done in a way that is free from stereotypical cultural and social bias? No one in the audience, which included other Asian American professionals, made any comments. In fact, here is the response to Keiko from an Asian American female friend who attended this forum and had discussed it with other Asian American women: "It made us uncomfortable to see two Asian professionals arguing. You should not have confronted an Asian male in front of a big group."

In this scenario, many Asian females saw the Asian male's emotion as acceptable while the Asian female's disagreement with the Asian male in public was perceived as inappropriate. Female assertiveness is perceived as aggression, even by Asian females, because of the double dosage of cultural and theological patriarchy.

In fact, Harriet Goldhor Lerner articulates that we do not even have terms that describe male anger as negative, while many terms exist for female anger.[13] Female anger is trivialized while male anger is legitimized, and theological patriarchy silences Asian Christian females once again. We are not only culturally homeless, but we are theologically homeless as well.

Angry Women Are Threatening

If we are guilty, depressed, or self-doubting, we stay in place. We do not take action except against our own selves, and we are unlikely to be agents of personal and social change. In contrast, angry women may change and challenge the lives of us all, as witnessed in the past decade of feminism. Change causes anxiety and is difficult business for everyone, including those of us who are actively pushing for it. Thus, we, too, learn to fear our own anger not only because it brings about the disapproval of others but also because

---

13. Harriet Goldhor Lerner, *Dance of Anger: A Woman's Guide to Changing the Patterns of Intimate Relationships* (New York: Harper & Row, 1985), 2.

it signals the necessity for change in ourselves. Is my anger legitimate? Do I have a right to be angry? What good will it do? These questions are excellent ways of silencing ourselves and shutting off our anger.[14]

Lerner stresses that the denial of anger paralyzes the ability to be in touch with one's power to be because anger is a signal of the violation of one's being. Lerner's "challenge of anger" relates to the Asian American women's condition: "Our anger may be a signal that we are doing more and giving more than we can comfortably do or give. Or our anger may warn us that others are doing too much for us, at the expense of our own competence and growth."[15]

Women like Anne who openly express their anger at men are especially suspect. While affirming anger as a legitimate feeling, Lerner warns us about venting our anger. Venting anger only consumes our energy, pushing us toward rigid stagnation rather than toward clarifying and growth-producing effects on ourselves and others.[16]

Is the Woman's Place in the Kitchen?

Asian American women's folk wisdom explains that the way to gain power in the church is through the pastor's stomach:

> At the church, Pastor Chung is surrounded by ladies in their forties and fifties who constantly serve food and wait on him. These women in return gain informal power in the church through their influence on the pastor. They often change decisions that are made at congregational, committee, and even staff meetings. This creates conflict and chaos at all levels of the church.

What is the legitimate role of a woman in the church? The women who have discovered the kind of informal power described above fall into the role of creating unnecessary church conflict, competing with one another in order to gain more power from the pastor. The

---

14. Ibid., 3.
15. Ibid., 1.
16. Ibid., 4.

lack of availability of legitimate power for women brings disease to an otherwise healthy congregational life.

This unhealthy power dynamic between the leadership and the female laity needs to be addressed in order for the church to model a healthier family dynamic. Specifically, females need to be given legitimate voices and roles in the life of the church.

Violence

When verbal challenges have no effect, the result is sometimes the explosion of violence. May describes violence in the physical dimension as a failure of reasoning or persuasion.[17] But violence does not necessarily need to be physical to be experienced as a violation.

Karen is an extremely logical person. A second-generation Chinese American, she shares how her church leadership is dealing with her and her ministry:

> I have applied for an internship at the Chinese church where I attend. The church does not know where to place me because I do not fit the categories for children's ministry or youth work. Merely by being in seminary, I have been labeled as a feminist, an aggressive woman trying to invade "man's territory," or I am looked down upon as corrupted by American society, having strayed from Chinese values and proper ways of behaving as a "good Chinese woman."

An advisor to various pastoral search committees for Asian American churches as well as other churches in his denomination (which is actually supportive of women in ministry) has often asked some of these committees if they have considered or would consider female candidates. The frequent responses are, "The thought never even occurred to us"; and "Are there any?" When asked what they would do if given a female candidate to consider, the committee members have often said, "I don't know."

At a gathering of people in ministry to American-born Chinese people in the Los Angeles area, among all the women in the group,

---

17. May, *Power and Innocence*, 43.

I was practically the only one who was not a pastor's wife. Being a married minister doesn't help either. I have a married friend in the seminary whose Asian American husband is reasonably supportive, but many people question her vocation and calling, asking why she needs to do "these things." Some accuse her of being selfish, even of depriving her husband of having children—certainly not conforming to the role of a "good Chinese" or "Asian" wife. Some also do not know "what to do with him," since most married couples in ministry fall into the category of joint ministry or of a man in ministry with a supportive wife.

What are churches going to do with the growing number of female Asian American seminarians? Whether single or married, Asian American women leaders face a Catch-22 reality both within the church and out in the world. It feels more painful when the church treats us as if we are from Mars. This is inhumane treatment of members of the body of Christ.

Catch-22

An Asian American female teacher in a Christian college was excluded from her own people's gathering, sponsored by the Asian American males on campus. They completely shut her out of the planning process. When she later found out, she decided to share her idea for the event with the school official who was in charge of this particular gathering. Because of the reasonable nature of her idea, the official agreed to implement it. But at the actual gathering, the plan never materialized. Later, she ended up being labeled as one who "wants a prominent place in every gathering." This characterization was spread by the official and an Asian American male.

How are women on the front lines supposed to figure out when the dominant cultural group is going to project its image of Asian women onto us and expect us to conform to its rules? Having an Asian American woman's face can be very confusing in the white workplace, where gender equality is pervasive externally (in the form of rhetoric) but not internally. It is like being in an invisible war zone. At least in Asian American churches there are blatant signs and discussions about gender inequality everywhere that require no second guessing.

A twofold stigma of Asian American professional women occurs when white society embraces Asian and Anglo patriarchy in its attitude toward the female. The Asian American male's chauvinistic influence on the dominant power holder (the white male) excludes female input in order to be "culturally correct." Furthermore, both males interpret the female's desire for inclusion as a hunger for power.

When the Asian American teacher mentioned above wanted to be included in her own ethnic gathering at school, the power elite excluded her. Then, the dominant power structure blamed her for not being supported by her own community. When she has opportunities to utilize her expertise, she is told she is not experienced enough. When it comes to her less-experienced areas, she is then measured by different criteria.

Does My Culture Count?

Janet, the teacher's seminarian friend, is upset with the denial of who she is in the curriculum at the seminary where the multiculturalism rhetoric is at its peak:

> I am so angry at being stereotyped from both sides. My question never makes it as a question. I always have to listen to an answer that is not about my question. I feel violated.

Should a desire to be included be a crime against the status quo? This cry for inclusion, this cry for the power to be, is left unanswered. A false answer is attempted, one that labels the crier as "pushy." After the cry sifts through the patriarchal power grid as a hunger for power, it boomerangs back on the one who cries out and leaves her wounded by her own cry. This is worse than a cry that falls on deaf ears, because the victim is blamed. This "blaming the victim" syndrome is at the root of much Asian American female suffering.

Shared Stories Build Community

The sharing of our stories is the beginning of discovering ourselves and of connecting ourselves with others. Once we see ourselves in others and others in ourselves through our shared stories, our perceptions become enlarged and we realize that we are all marginal. This enlargement of perception through mutual affirmation opens the way for the building of community in diversity.

In sharing our stories to promote the building of community, theological identity is crucial. Theology is never done in a vacuum but always in the context of everyday life. Beneath our gender disparity lies a theological fallacy that alienates not only women but also men, because those who inflict pain are violated in their humanity as much as those who receive pain. However, in sharing our humanity, we encounter others' stories, and others become us. In order for Asian American women's integrity as human beings to be restored so that we may find our place in our own community as well as in the larger community, a gender-inclusive theology needs to be lived out at the congregational level. It is time for Asian American churches to embrace the lonely cry of Asian American women on the front lines.

To carry out this noble task, the exclusive either/or paradigm needs to be shifted to the both/and paradigm. Understanding occurs when we are in dialogue with different perspectives. Ironically and fortuitously, Asian concepts can provide some of the resolution to the problem of male power over female powerlessness. A fresh application of the circle of harmony found in yin and yang suggests complementarity, mutuality, and reciprocity. The both/and perspective, in which males and females complement one another and bring out the fullness of God's image, may open the way for better dialogue between race, gender, and class. As we begin to understand the plight of frontier women with the triple interlocking web of injustice, we will avoid hasty, narrow, reductionist evaluations.

We also need to read the biblical stories afresh in order to sort out the cultural baggage of long-held Western paradigms of theology and sort through our Eastern paradigms so that we may balance and expand our theological journey. This theological journey is for everyone—people of different cultures and individual uniqueness that fulfill the image of God.

Asian American women are very concerned about the connections between personal experience and theology. Theology has to be a lived-out discipline in the power of the Holy Spirit, which ought to build not divide the community. This requires a paradigm shift in the way we do our theologizing. We all need to be story sharers in order to understand one another. As the biblical stories weave into our stories, we find meaning in the fragmented post-modern world of urban wastelands. We become connected. Furthermore, by creating community, our fragmented reality moves from theological first-aid to the healing of wounds. Through intense struggles, Asian American women strive to make a whole out of fragmented parts.

Let the weaving together of our stories begin.

Imagining a Yinist Embodiment of Asian American Churches

In this final chapter, I imagine a more equal pulpit in Asian American churches, one that reflects the wholeness of the body of Christ. Despite several waves of feminism and more recent discourses on postcolonial and ecofeminism in academia, male dominance persists in pulpits on Sunday. Thus, many churches, Asian American churches in particular, remain largely patriarchal in structure and theological orientation. The exclusion of women's voices from the pulpit continues to marginalize women, relegating us to second-class status and perpetuating the masculinization of Christianity. Gender inclusivity in the pulpit would facilitate the wholeness and equality of both genders, and such an inclusion would result in a healthy body of Christ. I dare to imagine it implemented widely across mainline and evangelical churches in the United States.

For too long, Christian pulpits have been monopolized by men, thus normalizing and propagating the masculinization of Christianity. This pattern is even more pronounced in contemporary Asian American churches whose pastors espouse the complementarian model of white male megachurch pastors.[1] For example, my husband and I led a college and young adult ministry in 1985 for a conservative Korean immigrant church in Los Angeles. I was the only female on the pastoral staff, but nobody questioned my preaching as a woman. It wasn't until after we left the church that this situa-

---

1. Complementarianism is the view that men and women have different but complementary roles to play in religious life, marriage, and other realms.

tion came into question. Elder Sam, then the education elder, called me one day in puzzlement: "I cannot understand young college students today. They are turning down a female candidate for the college ministry. They said that women cannot preach and lead men." Obviously, elder Sam, a first-generation Korean American, was not familiar with the gospel according to John Piper, John MacArthur, Tim Keller, and Rick Warren.

Although some mainline denominations have made strides in attracting more women to the pulpit, these strides have not been matched in evangelical and independent churches. In general, evangelical churches are not influenced by the mainline denominations, but instead follow the lead of American megachurches and complementarian leaders. Under predominantly male-centered pulpits, women—the majority population of such churches—find themselves facing the choice of either yielding to masculine authority and power or exiting from the church altogether. In addition, ethnic churches are even less prone to hiring women clergy—including women who may have come of age in those churches. Thus, many women of color, both ordained and candidates alike, choose to serve in predominantly Euro-American churches. Unless ethnic church pulpits become more equitable, the patriarchal culture of these churches will continue to marginalize the voices of the majority of their congregants. This marginalization further alienates women leaders and potential leaders who then dis-assimilate from the dominant male leadership culture. Meanwhile, the churches themselves will likely continue to lose women congregants.

On the rare occasions that women clergy are hired, they are paid less than their male counterparts. This economic imbalance further disempowers women and results in the continued silencing of women's voices. Despite their numerical majority, women congregants who internalize patriarchal culture can appear to gladly surrender their voice and remain in the pews. Meanwhile, many who desire gender equity exit the church because of perceived irrelevance; this is especially true of younger women and even men. This phenomenon adds to the rise of the "dones" and "nones"[2] and will

---

2. See, for example, Becka Alper, "Why America's 'Nones' Don't Iden-

continue to have an effect on the socio-political fabric of the United States.

Becoming a more inclusive body, then, requires the unmasking of this internalized evangelical narrative shaped by patriarchal epistemology. Although politics are ubiquitous and notorious, rarely do we learn how to be as shrewd as Jesus taught his disciples to be before commissioning them. Yet, many evangelical women remain either naïve to shrewdness or engaged in futile power mongering. Navigating systems of power requires a sophisticated skillset that Asian American women often lack because they have been largely excluded from decision-making processes. This exclusion creates a professional gap between Asian American women and men in churches and seminaries. Thus, women continue to be generally unaware of how to negotiate and navigate power dynamics.

Gendered Authority in the Church

A male-gendered pulpit, with its symbolic and discursive power of male authority over women, harms the body of Christ and reinforces male dominance in the life of the church as well as the family. Many women of color experience a chasm between seminaries and churches. Many Asian American pastors' biggest influencers are Anglo-European megachurch pastors who practice a male-centric Christianity. Sometimes, when the size of the church is still small, women are given access to full leadership. But the minute the numbers grow, they block women's access to the pulpit. Therefore, the need to reeducate pastors and community leaders to be more gender inclusive and to practice power sharing is greater today. While more progressive churches age and decline, more conservative independent churches disproportionately attract Asian Americans into their pews as conservative megachurches plant their franchises.

Unless gender equality is modeled in the pulpits, the transformation of patriarchal church culture, particularly within ethnic churches, is not feasible. When voices and representations are barred, the fullness of the body of Christ weakens, and public wit-

---

tify with a Religion," Pew Research Center, August 8, 2018, www.pew research.org.

ness wanes. Addressing the church's authority in the world from an Asian American perspective is as challenging now as it was more than three decades ago when C.-S. Song described it as trying to nail a theological stick in the air.[3] Unlike the mainstream's debate over Christianity and cultural establishment, and impending cultural disestablishment, the urgent issues for the hybrid Asian American remains reconciling innate Asian cultural heritage and Western Christianity.

Conversations about gender inequality in the church have the potential to reach much further than the simple visibility of women's bodies in the pulpit. "The pulpit" becomes a symbol for the priorities of the church. Addressing the visibility issue enables communities to address related and intersectional issues such as labor equity, work-life balance, and so on.

The consequences of continuing the male-centric pulpits are enormous. Women clergy will continue to experience the limiting of their sacred gifts and will continue to suffer the injustice of unequal access and pay. Meanwhile, maintaining a male-gendered reality in the church injures the body of Christ in many ways:

- robbing the body of Christ of the fullness of the gospel
- silencing the voices of gifted women preachers
- continuing the masculinization of Christianity, thus imposing on it a contingent and particular ideology that presents itself as universal
- losing younger generations of women leaders
- modeling deep structural power inequality in a culture of blatant disparities
- increasing violence against women and women's bodies within the church and in the world

For these reasons, constructing an inclusive Asian American ecclesiology is vital.

At the core of Asian American ecclesiology lie two convergent pieties—the Confucian filial piety of the East and the evangelical

---

3. Choan-Seng Song, *Third-Eye Theology* (Maryknoll, NY: Orbis Books, 1979), 5.

piety of the West. The Chinese concept of filial piety (*Hsiao*), reverence for parents, is considered the basis of all right human relations and is commonly shared by the East Asian cultures and the Vietnamese. Meanwhile, evangelical piety originates from the German Lutheran religious movement of the seventeenth and eighteenth centuries and emphasizes joyous abandon, heartfelt devotion, ethical sensitivity, and social outreach. It is ecumenically and experientially inclined rather than strictly sacramental or dogmatic.[4]

Why do so many Asian American Christians find an anchoring home in the evangelical expression of Christian faith? Interestingly, one can see how reverence for parents can be easily translated to devotion to God as the Father. Consequently, the gendered Confucian family structure based on father–son kinship is assured, rather than challenged, by the evangelical gender hierarchy. This assurance can be of great comfort in the face of the numerous uncertainties of life as immigrants. In fact, the Bible has many references to the significance of the firstborn son, paralleling the structure of filial piety. "'You are my Son; today I have become your Father.' Or again, 'I will be his Father, and he will be my Son.' And again, when God brings his firstborn into the world . . .'" (Heb 1:5, 6).

As Asian American immigrants settle in a foreign land, the church functions as a home away from home and an extended family based on the strong ethos of filial piety. While evangelical piety offers devotion to God, the Father, filial piety views the pastor as the person with authority by position and congregants as children who are expected to show obedience to the spiritual authority of their leaders. Initially, the convergence of the two dispositions—filial piety and evangelical piety, led to the growth of Asian American churches. However, this growth often does not survive the first generation as conflict rips the church apart. The old cultural ethos weakens in the face of American culture, democracy, individualism, and freedom. With the congregants' accomplishment of upward mobility comes the changing of the ecclesial subculture that poses a clash between the ascribed and the achieved authority. The power struggle between the congregants and the leaders within the church

---

4. F. Ernest Stoeffler, *The Rise of Pietism* (Leiden: Brill, 1965), 2–23.

becomes more pronounced as the immigrant congregants seek more decision-making power rather than simply remaining obedient to the top-down decision-making system. Therefore, many sources of ecclesiastical conflict stem from this changing concept of authority, which weakens its cohesive understanding in a new context. Simultaneously, lacking internalization of the American civic culture, first-generation Asian American churches face a collision course when it comes to negotiating parliamentary polity procedure. Consumed with internal conflict, the Asian American church's authority to be a witness in the world at times appears tarnished except for when the power of the Holy Spirit transcends the frailty of human nature.

Another notable aspect is the vacuum of the gospel's public witness in the arena of social justice. It is silent about race and gender issues despite the congregants' experiences of discrimination because of race and gender differences. The church's silence, due to an other-worldly interpretation of the gospel, perpetuates rather than transforms gender inequality and inequity in the church.

According to Sally K. Gallagher's research on evangelical identity as subculture, several areas characterize it: "spiritual authority and leadership, submission, decision making, parenting, and household labor and distinguished subtle differences between men's 'being responsible *for*' from 'taking responsibility.'"[5]

Whereas the postmodern context readily opens up a rare opportunity for groups excluded by the Judeo-Christian culture, many Asian American churches are confined to the modernity paradigm rooted in the dualistic separation of private and public, sacred and profane, this world and the other world. Under this dichotomous belief system, theological and social paradigms are compartmentalized. Furthermore, Western and Confucian fundamentalism find a comfortable nesting ground in evangelical Christianity that stresses piety, clearly defined truth, and the literal interpretation of Scripture, thus mirroring the influence of modern missionaries in Asia. Interestingly, both Confucianism and evangelicalism

---

5. Sally K. Gallagher, *Evangelical Identity and Gendered Family Life* (New Brunswick, NJ: Rutgers University Press, 2003), 104.

share a commonality in "piety," in that the former stresses "filial piety," and the latter the "German piety" that birthed the evangelical movement.

In his *Pia Desideria* (1675), Philipp Jakob Spener proposed a "heart religion" to replace the dominant "head religion" (Stoffler, 1971). Pietism began with religious meetings in Spener's home. The movement grew rapidly, enabled by August Hermann Francke (1663–1727), who made the new University of Halle a center for Pietism.[6]

Nikolaus Ludwig von Zinzendorf, a student of Francke and Spener's godson, further spread the movement. His Moravian Church inspired evangelical awakenings throughout Europe and North America in the eighteenth and nineteenth centuries. John Wesley and Methodism were greatly influenced by Pietism.

This brings us to today, where the majority of Asian American congregations belong to evangelical traditions, and the *implicit* practice of Confucian filial piety. I believe a yinist imagination of the churches can balance this extremely exclusive ecclesiology and move us toward the fullness of the body of Christ.

Taoism and Process Theology

The contrast between Eastern and Western philosophy, becoming versus being, breaks down in Alfred Whitehead's process thought. According to Whitehead, "Everything that exists is an experiencing subject as this subjectivity becomes in the process of the movement from disjunction to conjunction."[7] Thus, the parallel between Lao Tzu and Whitehead lies in their emphasis on becoming, intuition, and creativity. These fall under the category of yin in Taoism. In contrast to highly yang-principled Confucianism, scholars categorize Taoism as yinish.

---

6. Linda Edwards, *A Brief Guide to Beliefs: Ideas, Theologies, Mysteries, and Movements* (Louisville, KY: Westminster John Knox Press, 2001), 358.

7. Ernest L. Simmons Jr., "Mystical Consciousness in a Process Perspective," *Process Studies* 14, no. 1 (Spring 1984): 8.

There is room for debate, however, as to whether Whitehead's interpretation of Aristotle's substance is correct. Some scholars, such as Leonard Eslick and Charles Hartshorne, are suspicious as to whether Aristotle's view on substance was as mechanistic as Whitehead assumed.[8] Due to the space and the nature of this chapter, I will focus on the fact that both Taoism and Whitehead's process thought share their commonality in organic and polemic views.

The pioneer of process theology, John B. Cobb Jr., shares Taoistic epistemology as he challenges "static views of authority, of the church, and of God."[9] Unlike the classic monopolar view of God, which is absoluteness, process theology advocates a dipolar view of God. It conceptualizes God in two poles—"the *actual pole* of God" and "a *potential pole* to God's being which is beyond the world." Ronald Nash interprets the two poles of God as follows:[10]

God's Primordial Nature	God's Consequent Nature
transcendent	contingent
abstract	concrete
necessary	contingent
transcendent	immanent
eternal	temporal
potential	actual
one	many
infinite	finite
cause	effect
absolute	relative
immutable	mutable

8. James W. Felt, "Whitehead's Misconception of 'Substance' in Aristotle," *Process Studies* 14, no. 4 (Winter 1985): 225.

9. John B. Cobb, "Points of Contact: Process and Liberation Theology in Matters of Faith and Justice," in *Process Studies* 14, no. 2 (Summer 1985): 124.

10. Ronald Nash, ed., *Process Theology* (Grand Rapids, MI: Baker Book House, 1987), 19.

The dipolar concept of God in process theology corresponds to the concept of "TAO," that is Truth Above Oneself and Truth Among Ourselves.

> Tao, the subtle reality of the universe
> cannot be described.
> That which can be described in words
> is merely a conception of the mind.
> Although names and descriptions have been applied to it,
> the subtle reality is beyond the description. [11]

Truth above oneself and among ourselves provides a parallel to a transcendent and immanent God. In the concept of *Tao Te Ching,* there is no separation of theory from action. *Tao* means the integral truth of the universe; *Te* means the virtuous application of such high, subtle knowledge; and *Ching* means serious spiritual guidance. In Taoism, knowledge and application are not separable. Therefore, it can balance dichotomized structure and theological education. Taoism and process theology as epistemology can offer hope of recovering the broken link between humanity and nature through holistic education.

Nevertheless, I am not completely in agreement with Taoism and process theology. In response to critics, Cobb readily admits the need to connect process theology with liberation theology. He is rightly concerned about the class gap in education. Cobb writes:

> education in general as it is now institutionalized widens the gap between the rich and the poor. Even where it is made available to the poor, it rarely functions to help them deal with their own problems. . . . This means that the high valuation of science and education, so widespread across the world, is an expression of the interests of the rich and powerful.[12]

---

11. Hua-Ching Ni, *The Complete Works of Lao Tzu: Tao Te Ching & Hau Hu Ching,* rev. ed. (Los Angeles: Seven Star Communications, 1995), 7.
12. Cobb, "Points of Contact," 124–41.

Bridging the Educational Gap

In bridging educational gaps, one cannot help but raise questions not only about educational perspective but also methodology. Can an organic perspective be contained in a mechanistic container?

There are lively discussions on theological education today because theological education is in crisis because of its inability to adapt fast enough to a changing culture. In North America, numerous articles were produced dealing with the very identity of the seminary and of theological education. Is the seminary a graduate school or a vocational school? Regretfully, one cannot help but be reminded of the fact that it is neither a graduate school nor a vocational school in its orientation. Meanwhile, some feel that divinity schools within universities are more effective than specialized seminaries. This ambiguous in-betweenness creates more confusion with regard to student expectations. Students expect that they are enrolled in the seminary to be equipped as ministers. In this milieu comes a refreshing voice of holistic education, Parker Palmer, who writes,

> The mind immersed in prayer no longer thinks in order to divide and conquer, to manipulate and control. Now, thinking becomes an act of love, a way of acknowledging our common bonds and assuming our rightful role in the created community.[13]

In his dialogue with a political theologian, John Cobb quotes Johann Baptist Metz as stating, "the primary problem of Christianity today is not that its doctrines are unclear or out of contact with current scientific and philosophical thought, but that its practice is not faithful."[14] Cobb readily admits the lack of effort in process theology to bridge theory and practice. Meanwhile, Father

---

13. Parker J. Palmer, *To Know as We Are Known: Education as a Spiritual Journey* (San Francisco: Harper & Row, 1993), 11–12.

14. John B. Cobb, *Process Theology as Political Theology* (Manchester, England: Manchester University Pres/Philadelphia: Westminster Press, 1982), 56.

Ben Beltran of the Smoky Mountain community in the Philippines experienced frustration with theological education because of its dichotomy between theory and practice. He sought solutions from living among the poor. He says, "We should not think that only theologians understand the Bible. We have not listened to the poor. Just because they are unlettered does not mean that the truths of the Bible cannot be revealed to them."[15]

There are few Father Bens in Korea, and thus we find that Korean theological education generally suffers from extreme polarization between theological perspective and its pedagogy. The Christian schism has blocked the power of dialogue when facing differences. Both religious and cultural fundamentalism have imprisoned the gospel within the four walls of Christian institutions. It is as if the water itself is so contaminated that anyone who enters into it is tainted.

Kim Min Ki, a musician and a dissident, wrote many antiwar and anti-military dictatorship songs. His songs were highly popular in South Korean political protests in the 1980s. Predictably, many of his songs were forbidden during the military regime. One of his songs in particular, "A Little Pond" (1972), embodies the mutual and interdependent ecosystems of yinist spirituality:

In a small pond along a deep mountain path
only black water welled up with no sign of life.
They say that long ago two beautiful gold fish
lived in this little pond
deep in the mountain.
One clear summer day the fish began to fight.
One floated above the water and its soft flesh decayed,
Soon the water decayed as well.
No living creature could live there again.

In a small pond along a deep mountain path
only black water welled up with no sign of life.

---

15. Jane Sutton, "Telling It on the Mountain," *World Vision Today* 4, no. 1 (Summer 1998).

The leaves once green fell one by one floating a small
ship on the pond and then sank deep in the water.
A lost flower deer wandered in the mountain and found the
    pond.
Upon drinking the water it quietly fell asleep.[16]

These lyrics were written during a dark time in Korea in the
1980s when many innocent students were imprisoned for protest-
ing the long-held military dictatorship. No voice against violent
oppression was allowed. Kim, a Korean Bob Dylan, courageously
proclaimed the truth with powerful metaphors, when the voices of
the truth were brutally crushed. The power held by the military was
confronted by Kim's armor-less voice. The extreme either/or lens of
win-or-lose reality was confronted with its dire consequences. The
poet turns our attention to the mutual and interdependent nature
of life whose sustainability depends on seeking the common good.
These lyrics graphically portray the interdependent nature of social
and ecological life against winner-takes-all destruction.

Similarly, Taoism was launched during a time of extreme corruption in China; the parallel is seen in today's economically driven
culture that endangers all living organisms. The *Tao Te Ching*
describes a society that lost common truth:

When people stray from the subtle way of universal nature,
    they can no longer perceive their own true nature.
Thus, they emphasize relative virtue.
When natural virtue is lost,
    society depends on the doctrine of humanism.
When humanity becomes corrupted,
    social and religious teachings appear
    and become powerful forces.
When social and religious teachings become corrupted,
    what is left behind is the empty shell
    of superficial ceremonies and artificial etiquette.

---

16. Kim Min Ki is a Korean folk singer and song writer who wrote the
lyrics and tunes. The English translation of the lyrics of "A Little Pond" is by
Young Lee Hertig.

When etiquette is emphasized,
  it is because people lack the simple qualities
  of fairness and kindness.
This is the starting point of people of confusion.[17]

Lao Tzu's teaching is significant in today's digital contexts that confuse people with the nonstop news cycles of one's choosing. The decline of the virtue of the common good leaves humanity with less common ground. Theological education is also under siege by technology and is crippled by the lack of holistic education. Consequently, we are in greater need for *Tao Te Ching*, which could offer a theological education that connects mind, body, and spirit.

A lifestyle grounded on extreme capitalism paralyzes the possibility of the common good. Against this extreme position, people show a hunger for spirituality. Unless the very glasses we see life through changes, the enrichment of humanity is not possible.

Feminists have long challenged the dichotomous epistemology of reason and intuition. Many cultural feminists, including Griffin and Leland, operate out of a gendered dualism of culture as masculine and nature as feminine. According to Leland, the masculine impulse is to "separate, divide, individuate, discriminate, dominate. The list of gender dichotomies includes objective/subjective, reason/intuition, patriarchy/matriarchy, public/private."[18] Judith Grant argues that cultural feminists are embracing a patriarchal definition of masculine and feminine dualism when they think they are advocating for women's status. The question Grant raises is worth our attention: "to what extent do these gendered dualisms themselves reflect and *reproduce* patriarchal social relations?"[19] Grant is rightly concerned about the problem of reason representing male and intuition representing female, thus reinforcing the dichotomy of masculinity and femininity.

---

17. Ni, *The Complete Works of Lao Tzu*, 53.
18. Quoted in Judith Grant, "I Feel Therefore I Am: A Critique of Female Experience as the Basis for a Feminist Epistemology," in *Feminism and Epistemology: Approaches to Research in Women and Politics*, ed. Maria J. Falco (New York: Haworth Press, 1987), 102–3.
19. Ibid.

This is where the yinist paradigm, based on Taoism, overcomes dualistic separation through its emphasis on balance and harmony both within and without:

> Human culture has polarized maleness with *yang* exclusively, and femaleness with *yin* exclusively. However, both male and female have *yin* and *yang* energies. *Yinist* feminism as theology of balance is twofold. First, *yin* and *yang* are found both in male and female. One reaches the fullness of humanity when he or she identifies with both *yin* and *yang* within himself or herself. Simultaneously, *yin* in male and *yin* in female are not the same. . . . Second, once the first point is reached, the extreme polarization of male as *yang* and female as *yin* will be balanced.[20]

"Our options limited by linear reductionism, we perceive reality as two opposite points on a line. Unable to find a synthesis or consider other alternatives, non-Tao people become trapped in the false dilemma of either/or."[21] Therefore, the yin and yang polarity "is not to be confused with the ideas of opposition. . . . The *yin-yang* principle is not, therefore, what we would ordinarily call a dualism, but rather an explicit duality expressing an implicit unity," writes Alan Watts in his last book on Taoism.[22] The duality, instead of dualism, offers nonlinear, nonoppositional lenses to work on the balance of social, cultural, and ecological relationships.

There has been a strong emphasis on practical theology in the West in the last decade or two. This need for practical theology stems from the dualistic separation of idea from being. Conversely, in the Eastern mind, the very essence of learning takes place when there is a fusion between the idea and being.

---

20. Young Lee Hertig, "The Asian American Alternative to Feminism: A *Yinist* Paradigm," in *Mirrored Reflections: Reframing Biblical Characters*, ed. Young Lee Hertig and Chloe Sun (Eugene, OR: Wipf & Stock, 2019), 19.

21. Diane Dreher, *The Tao of Inner Peace: A Guide to Inner and Outer Peace* (New York: HarperCollins, 1990), 7–8.

22. Alan Watts and Al Chung-Liang Huang, *Tao, The Watercourse Way* (New York: Pantheon Books, 1975), 19, 26.

John McKnight raises a skeptical question referring to educational institutions. As "modern universities as institutions have become commercial gatekeepers whose grades select the elites, who will control the future?" He asks, are professors servants who depend upon deficiency and control rather than competence and community?[23] Such unilateral education, divorced from the contexts of the learners, falls under the dualism that separates knowledge from realities beyond the ivory tower. Thus, it lacks power to bridge, reinforces elitism, and is anti-incarnational as supratheology.

Heart Matters

There exists an urgent need to bridge theology and ministry in the current context where the two have been disconnected. Educator Parker Palmer brings soul back to education and inspires us in the way theological education ought to be: "to teach is to create a space in which obedience to truth is practiced."[24] Palmer, through the emphasis of transformational education, brings mind and heart together in seeking truth.

The word "heart" is mentioned more than one thousand times in the Bible. Heart (*leb*) in the Hebrew understanding represents a person's center for both physical and emotional-intellectual-moral activities. The condition of a person's heart measures the quality of the life, activities, and relationships s/he imparts: "Guard your heart, for everything you do flows from it" (Proverbs 4:23); "Blessed are the pure in heart, for they will see God" (Matthew 5:8); "For out of the overflow of the heart, the mouth speaks" (Matthew 12:34). Jesus, in his ministry, emphasized the condition of the heart of his followers. He perfectly demonstrates a pastoral capacity for extending deep empathy and connection with diverse people.

A pastoral leader requires opportunities to attend to the condition of one's inner being, to be guided in honest and redeeming soul

---

23. John McKnight, *The Careless Society: Community and Its Counterfeits* (New York: Basic Books, 1995).

24. Palmer, *To Know as We Are Known*, xii.

formation, to reflect on one's capacity—and one's limitations—for extending compassion, imagination, intelligence, and gifts for the service of God and the community of God. When a pastor finds her-/himself in regular engagement with such reflection and formation, a thriving ministry marked by heart-to-heart connections, as modeled by Christ, emerges in preaching, pastoral care, and missions.

I cannot emphasize enough the importance of cultivating one's heart to tap into the heartbeat of God in ministry. Theological education's approach to equipping leaders deemphasizes pastoral care while focusing on their fragmented knowledge base. However, pastoral leadership requires communion with God and with the people of God. John T. Ford describes Christians as pilgrims accompanied by Christ and their fellow believers. The Latin etymology of *companion* refers to breaking bread together: *com* ("with") and *panis* ("bread"). Embedded in this view of vocational journey is the sacramental expression of companionship. Recognizing one's need for an abiding communion with God and for authentic companionship with others is a vital mark of a pastor's capacity for leading a thriving and sustaining ministry.

In an era of accelerations, digitization, and constant change, opportunities for cultivating the kind of pastoral leadership necessary for thriving ministries do not naturally present themselves. Unless an intentional community is formed in which pastors are afforded the extended time necessary for honest self and soul formation, pastoral leaders, who often find themselves isolated from one another, succumb to the demands of their ministry and unrelenting expectations for church growth.

While all persons preparing for and partaking in the pastoral vocation face challenges of discovering authentic integrity in one's personal and professional identities, persons of minority ethnic heritages have an additional layer of cultural complexities to unpack. North American seminaries fail to reflect the complexity in the professional identity formation of ministers. Assumptions about normative human experiences, perspectives, and hermeneutics afford little room to recognize the value of one's particular agency, narrative, and imagination. Additionally, seminary education holds

cognitive forms of knowledge processing as its normative epistemology.

The hierarchy of knowledge processing and construction upheld
in seminary classrooms fails to maximize the various funds of
knowledge that come from emotional, spiritual, and relational wis-
doms. Consequently, there is a need for an embodied theological
vision and practice to complement seminary degree work in order
to shift the expectations of learners from passive spectator to active
participant, and to establish a holistic theological education that
accompanies the transforming of mind/body/spirit.

Imagining a more inclusive embodiment of Asian American
churches, I propose a "PastoraLab" that reflects a yinist embodiment. PastoraLab will be uniquely positioned to build a wide network of seasoned pastors of both women and men to shine their
wisdom in guiding pastors for sustainable ministry.

PastoraLab for Leadership Formation

Considering the large Asian American population in Southern
California within several Asian American megachurches, it is noteworthy that both denominational and seminary bookstores do not
carry Don Nakanishi's *Asian American Leadership*.[25] A strong
implication from this "chasing down the book" experience is that
ethnic minority literature is still marginalized by mainstream marketing—including book distribution, purchase, and curricula. In
contrast to the electronic book market, the traditional bookstore
still remains highly monocultural. The online medium has made
strides in making ethnic minority writings easily accessible. However, the resources on Asian American leadership in particular are
grossly underrepresented. To fill this vacuum, there is a need for
learning and belonging in order for Asian American pastors to participate in the kind of personal and communal formation (and reformation) that is at the foundation of a thriving ministry.

PastoraLab can be a third space of Asian American yinist
hermeneutical formation through engagement across ethnicity,

25. Don Nakanishi, *Asian American Leadership: A Reference Guide*
(Santa Barbara, CA: Mission Bell Media, 2015).

generation, and gender (EGG). It could provide an intersectional space that embodies gender equality and equity in Asian American churches. By providing a series of peer listening sessions, mutual inquiry, communal forums, and intergenerational mentor relationship engagements, I believe change is possible for pastors and churches.

In Roy M. Oswald and Arland Jacobson's book *The Emotional Intelligence of Jesus* (2015), the cruciality of the hearts of pastors is emphasized. As such, I believe the following components are essential for pastoral ministry: (1) self-awareness; (2) self-management—adaptability, emotional self-control; (3) social and organizational awareness; and (4) relationship cultivation—conflict management, coach and mentor relationship, influence, and teamwork. Another important and rare attribute among pastoral practice is Distributive Leadership (DL), a concept growing rapidly in the United Kingdom. DL highlights that "in order to be effective, there needs to be balanced 'hybrid configuration' of Distributive Leadership practice. In the Asian American context, Distributive Leadership resides in (re)constructing leader–follower identities, mobilizing collective engagement and challenging or reinforcing traditional forms of organization."[26]

I look forward to creating such a space for the embodiment of yinist spirituality that practices gender equality and equity for a fuller body of Christ so that it may gain authority to be a public witness in this challenging world today.

---

26. Richard Bolden, ""Distributed Leadership in Organizations: A Review of Theory and Research," *International Journal of Management Reviews* 13 (2011): 251–69.